R.E. OLDS:
AUTOMOTIVE PIONEER & YACHTSMAN

By

Peter J. Stephens

AUTOTOGO PUBLISHING CO.
2018

b

R.E. OLDS:
AUTOMOTIVE PIONEER & YACHTSMAN

DEDICATION

TO DEBBIE

I wish to thank my wife, Deborah Olds Anderson Stephens, for her love and support in encouraging me to write this book with its unique perspective of her great grandfather. She continues to amaze me with her dedication and devotion to keeping the memory of R.E. Olds alive. This book is a small gesture of my love and support for her.

TABLE OF CONTENTS
(Names of Yachts & Boats listed)

Acknowledgements		v
Preface		vi
The Olds Family		xi
List of Photographs		xv
The Yachts of R.E. Olds		xviii

Chapter 1   **The Early Years: 1880 to 1903**   1
- *Mary Ann*
- *Little Mayflower*
- *East Wind*
- *Jumbo*
- *REO Bird (I & II)*

Chapter 2   **The Glory Years: 1904 to 1920**   20
- *Rochester*
- *REOMAR*
- *REOMAR II*
- *REOPASTIME*
- *REOLA*
- *REOLA II*

Chapter 3   **The Transition Years: 1921 to 1940**   51
- *REOMAR III*
- *The Flying Cloud*
- *REOMAR IV*
- *REOMETTA*
- *METTAMAR*
- *NAYADA*

Other:
- *Captain Alfred Brow*
- *Al Capone*

Chapter 4   **The Final Years: 1941 to 1950:**   96
- *Mary Ann*
- *REOLA III*
- *Sealark*
- *METTMAR II*
- *REOLA IV*

Chapter 5	**Oldsmar**	**104**
Chapter 6	**Family Photographs**	**109**

ACKNOWLEDGEMENT

Many individuals contributed to the knowledge and spirit of this book. If you walk away after reading this book feeling you have a better understanding and awareness of R.E. & Metta Olds, their lives, contributions and their yachts, it will be due to those people that helped with this book.

The great grandchildren of R.E. & Metta Olds, all cousins of the author's wife, provided stories and photographs which made the Olds' approachable and relevant. Ed Roe Jr., Tom Roe, Phil Fouke and Clela Gray were very supportive and extremely helpful in their edits and comments. I deeply appreciate time they gave towards this project.

The R.E. Olds Transportation Museum in Lansing, Michigan is home to a great repository of information about Olds and vehicles from his career. Executive Director Bill Adcock, who does an outstanding job presenting Olds' accomplishments, was very helpful in his comments and support. Museum Historian Dave Pfaff who is among the most knowledgeable individuals about Olds and Lansing Transportation was especially helpful. His comments and suggestions kept me on track. This book is an outgrowth of a six foot by four foot timeline of R.E. & Metta Olds' life the author prepared for the museum; Dave Pfaff's detailed review of the timeline was extremely helpful. I also deeply appreciate the time both men took to read and edit the draft of this book.

The late Joe Merli who best represented the spirit and creativity of R.E. Olds was very encouraging in the early planning stages of the book. While he never lived to see the finished book, I hope it measures up to his standard for excellence. His re-creations of Olds' early cars, now on exhibit at the R.E. Olds Transportation Museum, are of a caliber of workmanship that would have made R.E. Olds proud.

Last and certainly not least, I want to thank my sons Matt & Gregg Stephens. Matt, helped with technology issues and Gregg, who truly did a yeoman's job transcribing the ship's logs, which was essential to understanding life aboard the yachts from the Olds' and crew's perspective.

Author's note:

100% of the purchase price of this book will go to the R.E. Olds Transportation Museum as a fund raiser. The cost of publishing the book has been paid for by the author. The R. E. Olds Transportation Museum and the author thank you for your purchase and donation to the Museum.

Preface

"Many a forenoon have I stolen away, preferring to spend thus the most valued part of the day; for I was rich, if not in money, in sunny hours and summer days, and spend them lavishly; nor do I regret that I did not waste more of them in the workshop or the teacher's desk"
Walden

Thoreau

R.E. Olds was a fascinating figure in history and a major contributor to the American automobile industry and its dominance in the world. For all his accomplishments and philanthropic accomplishments, he is little remembered or acknowledged any more. His own beloved hometown of Lansing, Michigan rarely acknowledges the man who singlehandedly had the biggest impact on the development of the city as a center of commerce and industry. His quiet but effective generosity impacted thousands of Lansing residents over many decades.

In his day, he was often given many titles: The Great Teacher, Father of the Popular Priced Car and the Father of the American Auto Industry. His innovations for the assembly line, mass production of cars, marketing of cars and establishing the low priced car for the masses set the pattern for the automobile industry. He believed that there would be a new class of workers with more disposable income with time for recreation with their families. His grand real estate plan of Oldsmar, Florida was going to showcase his idea of a planned development for the emerging middle class. Olds often stated that "A car should be the child of necessity instead of the child of luxury."

Interestingly, his low priced car also appealed to the wealthy: The Queen of England, Mark Twain, Sir Thomas Lipton, Italy's Queen Helena, the Czar of Russia and Argentina's President were all purchasers of Curved Dash Olds.

For all his accomplishment and achievements, he remained a humble man, who loved his family, friends and life. His photographs always show a smiling man at peace. Could he have achieved more greatness and wealth, perhaps? But he reached a point in life where ever greater rewards were not as meaningful to him. His time with family and being on his yacht on the water held far greater satisfaction for him.

What is it that draws such a man to the water? Why is it that for ages mankind knowingly and willingly accepted risk, danger and certain death to explore and learn from what the oceans had to tantalizingly offer? Is it the adventure, the light & motion or is it a sense of tranquility that we derive from it?

R. E. Olds was a man who loved the water. As you will learn, he was drawn to it from the time of his youth. As a boy, he tried to create a new pump for the farm house. As a young man in Lansing, he built a boat and later gave rides to paying passengers on the Grand River. One of the paying passengers in those early days later became his wife. Later in life, he sought to cruise on his beloved yachts as a form of relaxation.

While there is no doubt that Olds was a hard worker as shown by his numerous patents, varied business interests and wide spread travels, he also delighted in his time away from "the office". He was a very social person and surrounded himself with likeminded people. He threw as much energy into their social life as he did his varied business interests.

His creativity and work ethic resulted in significant contributions to the nascent automobile manufacturing industry.

The initial period of the automotive industry is typically referred to as the Horseless Carriage era. Olds was the chief contributor during this period and was often willing to teach and guide those who wanted to get involved in the industry. He willingly shared his patents and knowledge. Olds' marketing practices set the standard for the emerging industry. Ford, who was not a key contributor during this period, learned about Olds' best practices, such as the assembly line and the use of outside suppliers, before becoming a force in his own right. The list of those who learned from Olds reads like a Who's Who®: Dodge, Leland, Buick, Durant, Ford, and Chapin.

Interestingly, the reason Detroit became the center of the American automobile industry was due to Olds, not Ford. Olds' plant in Detroit in 1900 was the first solely dedicated automobile manufacturing in Michigan, perhaps arguably the nation. Olds' subsequent decision to subcontract parts, for his newly created assembly line, to local manufacturers that solidified Detroit as "the" manufacturing center for automobiles. Olds had established Detroit and Michigan as a leading manufacturing center before Ford built his first car. It took Ford and his Model T until 1908 to become the volume leader.

By the end of the first decade of the 1900's, Olds' interest in the industry was waning and Ford rose to prominence. Ford and his innovations, building upon Olds and others, made him the leading automobile industrialist for the next ten years until the First World War.

After the First World War ended, the industry had matured to the point that the large corporations needed to be run by men of great intellect and power. Names such as Sloan, DuPont, Chrysler and Kettering were the leaders of this great industry. The automobile industry, which started only a few decades before, now positioned the United State as the leading industrial country in the world.

Starting in the early 1900's, the rigors of running multiple large companies must have taxed even R.E. Olds and his prodigious energy. His solution was to charter a boat in Florida and relax. That led to a series of yachts over the next 40 years.

R.E. also enjoyed his real estate. In 1926, he built a 17 room log lodge in Charlevoix which he named Oldswood. Every week during the summer, especially weekends, the lodge was filled with a crowd of guests. According to his grandson, R.E. Olds Anderson, there was no down time; R.E. Olds insisted that there must be some activity on going at all time! Lawn bowling, swimming (generally for the younger generations), singing, elaborate costume parties were just part of a typical stay at Oldswood. Elaborate invitations were created each winter with space left for the invitee's name and date they were expected to appear at Oldswood. Imagine the logistics of planning an entire year of social events, including cruises on the yachts, at multiple homes with hoards of visitors coming and going!

But, let's not forget about the yachts (the point of this book!). Every trip to visit Mr. & Mrs. Olds, wherever they were, also involved cruising time on a yacht and taking the family launch out for quick spins. The launches and runabouts were typically overloaded beyond what would meet modern day US Coast Guard regulations. It was all part of the Olds Party Theorem: invite as many people as the cottage or yacht could hold and then hold group activities where everyone participated in them. Olds was well known as an avid yachtsman. His moorings in various locations usually drew notice in local papers.

This book has no pretenses to be overly scholarly; rather it attempts to tell a story with previously undisclosed family history and photographs of a major aspect of the life of R.E. Olds from a different perspective. It is the hope that this book will provide additional insight on one of this country's most creative and interesting people, who is rapidly becoming lost to history.

During the course of the development of this book, additional drafts from other authors who were engaged to write Mr. Olds' biography were discovered in the family papers. These additional sources each provided nuggets of information and facts about Olds' life that had not been discovered previously.

Interestingly, there has been little attempt to document Olds' interest in yachts since his passing. Much of the blame can be placed squarely upon Olds himself as he made little effort to document his yachts and his family time aboard them beyond the standard ship's log and some family photographs. Olds' daughters Gladys & Bernice recorded family events and activities as they had developed an interest in family genealogy and an appreciation of the role their father played in history.

Much of the pictures and stories within come from the Olds family directly. Family photographs, unseen for generations, ships logs and family stories help create a very different picture of a very successful man. Olds was a master at creating ideas and businesses. He was a leading thought maker of his day. He had big ideas, whether it was saving the Great Lakes, elevating highways to relieve traffic congestion, or suggesting that newspapers stop publishing daily stock prices to stop people from being overly fixated on stock prices and the market! He also turned out to be exceptionally talented at innovations in yacht and engine design.

He also seemed to know when it was time to walk away either for a break or to separate himself from a business venture. Yet, he would soon create another great business idea which he would pour himself into but always maintained the ability to retreat to his beloved yachts.

Olds himself was a prolific yacht owner. He turned his yachts over fairly frequently: he owned a yacht for one trip (**REOMETTA**) yet kept the various **REOMAR's** for decades. He owned 15 documented yachts and boats (plus many more unrecorded), many of them around or greater than 100 feet plus countless smaller launches and runabouts. Given his engineering prowess and his creative mind, he was actively involved in the development of his yachts. It was not uncommon for him to be involved in the hull design, the development of engines (e.g. the diesels for **REOMAR IV**) and deciding the interior decorations of a given yacht. His long-time captain, Alfred Brow, once reflected that Olds' interest extended beyond the design & construction details; he was deeply interested in the mechanical operations including how trip nautical charts were prepared. Olds had a restless mind always looking for another challenge. As one project or invention went into general production, he seemed to lose interest, especially if it involved administration or day-to-day details. He relished in the unknown, the seemingly unsolvable. But he always had his balance: the water. That was his retreat, his safe zone.

In the end, his life was a remarkable one. Olds achieved great wealth which he shared generously with family, friends and charities. Olds always "picked up the tab" although he enjoyed portraying himself as a "tight miser". As several of his grandchildren said, he was a very generous man who enjoyed doing what he thought were small gestures for other people. His will left a long list of bequests to grandchildren, employees and friends. He left a large sum as an additional grant to the Ransom Fidelity Company, the oldest family foundation in Michigan, now known as the R.E. Olds Foundation. He firmly believed in donating to grassroots organizations that "didn't have corner offices". That foundation is still active today and still adheres to his same guiding principles. The foundation continues to support charities primarily in central Michigan. His final gestures were recognition of his appreciation towards a wonderful and satisfied life.

Much has been written about Olds' industrial life and his charitable undertakings; this is the story of the unknown chapter of his life: his love of yachting, the great satisfaction it brought him and the fascinating story of each yacht. It is telling that towards the end of his life when filling out yet another biographical form for an honor, he listed as his sole hobby: yachting.

The initial purpose of this book was to tell about Olds' love of yachting and his personal involvement in the development of each yacht. Through the use of the ship's log and family histories, it allowed the writer to recreate the trips and life of the Olds family over the decades.

However, it soon became apparent that the subsequent history of the yachts after Olds sold them was as fascinating or interesting as the time they were used by the Olds family. Olds' yachts were considered to be beautifully designed and creative for their use of space. Many of his yachts were purchased by people who were nearly as interesting as Olds himself. The subsequent owners were the last of a wealthy group who could afford to yacht as it was done during the first few decades of the Twentieth Century. Throw in a few rogue owners, an assassination attempt on a former Olds yacht against a prominent Ku Klux Klan member, rumors that Al Capone owned two of the Olds' yachts and you soon have an interesting secondary story as each yacht tells its own story.

Sadly, it appears that only one of Olds' many yachts or runabouts have survived: the Robinson Seagull commuter: **THE FLYING CLOUD**. The larger yachts ended up in service for World War II. Typically they were stripped of their adornments and staterooms were often converted into crew quarters. The smaller runabouts were simply lost to history.

Time to cast off and start the journey!

THE OLDS FAMILY

Ransom Olds life was a man shaped by many influences in his early years. Born in Geneva, Ohio (1864), young Olds was not highly educated in a formal sense, much of his learning was practical and structured. He attended school to learn the basics of reading, writing and arithmetic. He assisted his father, Pliny Fisk Olds, in the small foundry he ran in Lansing, MI. Ransom attended a local business school to learn accounting in order to help his father manage the small family business. The Olds family still owns young Ransom's high school physics textbook. His notes indicated an interest and desire to understand how machinery, specifically engines, worked. Young Ransom was not interested in sports as many young boys are but rather he was quite taken by engines and mechanical machines and the creative process.

> Historical footnote: *"Chalk Talkers" were a regular occurrence in the 1890's through the early part of the new century. Found typically at temperance and religious revivals, the speaker used chalk and a board to illustrate key points either by emphasizing words or figures. In 1889, a speaker came to Lansing, Michigan who fancied himself a better speaker than Thomas Nast (1840 – 1902) who was known as the "Father of the American Cartoon". Olds built for him a <u>revolving</u> easel, requiring "some parts that you hammered out on your anvil or turned in your lathe."*

There is a fairly complete Olds family tree that the author prepared for his wife and the other members of the Olds family going back to 1150 AD. The first Olds to come to America was Robert Olds, who came to the United States around 1665. Pliny's father was Jason, who was a Congregational minister. Jason was born in June, 1799 in Goshen, Massachusetts to Samuel and Persis Olds. Samuel Olds, Jason's father died when he was 14. Jason married Matilda Ford when he was 15, she was 20. By the age of 22, Jason had lost both parents and he now had 2 sons and a daughter. Pliny was born in 1828, in Hamilton, NY, when Jason was 29; he was the last child born to Jason & Matilda Olds. Pliny was born during his parent's move to Ohio. The family settled near Geneva, Ohio in the early 19th century from Massachusetts. Because of the nature of Pliny's adult work, it had always been assumed he was apprenticed at an early age.

Little is known about Pliny's early life, which is a shame given the impact he had not only on Ransom's life but the development of the company that became Oldsmobile. Pliny's career involved, at various times, being a farmer, blacksmith, manager of an ironworks facility, farmer, engineering pattern maker and then owner of a machine shop in Lansing, Michigan. Interestingly, family records indicate that Pliny attended Oberlin College in Ohio. A request submitted to Oberlin College did not find any record of Pliny's attendance. Pliny has received little credit for his role in the ultimate development of the Olds motorized vehicles. Pliny died at 80 from hemorrhaging of the lungs.

Pliny married Sarah Whipple in 1849. Even less is known about Sarah, other than she was born in 1824. Her family came from New York. Her father was Nathan Whipple, born in 1794 in Vermont. Her mother was Laura Mixer, born in 1797 in Massachusetts. They married in 1817 in Geauga, Ohio. The Olds family still has a sampler made by a young Laura Mixer in the family.

Gladys Olds Anderson, daughter of R.E. & Metta Olds, added comments in the margins of the Edson Olds book, The Olds Family", a family history of the various Olds family branches. Her comments were enlightening, humorous and insightful. She gave a personal perspective to what might had been a dry, internet fact based analysis.

After several unsuccessful careers, Pliny eventually traded his equity in a farm near Cleveland, Ohio for a house and an extra lot in Lansing, Michigan. In 1880, the family boarded a freight boat in Cleveland, Ohio that was advertising a $1.00 rate to Detroit, so the family traveled to Detroit for $6.00 or approximately $140 in 2018. The extra lot was sold for $2,500 later in 1880 to raise money to open a small machine engine shop on the west side of River Street, just south of Kalamazoo Street. Pliny used the proceeds to buy an old lathe, planer and an old engine boiler. The shop itself was quite small, only 18 feet by 36 feet. The resulting company, comprised of Pliny and Wallace, was essentially a repair shop handling small jobs. Occasionally, there was a custom job but that was very infrequent.

Numerous Olds biographies have mentioned the apparent fascination within the Olds family about Spiritualism. Spiritualism was a European phenomenon until the mid-1800's when it caught on in America. At its height, millions of Americans indulged in séances. People saw no conflict with their Christian beliefs. Communicating with the dead seemed normal and acceptable. One remaining gift of the Spiritualism movement is still with us today: the Ouija Board! The problems with séances is that it took too long to fully communicate messages to and from the dead. In 1886, The Associated Press reported that in an Ohio spiritualist camp, a board with letters, numbers and a pointing device was being successfully used to gather messages. But it was a group of businessmen, not spiritualists that got a patent and successfully marketed the new game, as the Patent Office referred to it.

Realistically, given the prominence of the Spiritualist movement and the popularity of séances, undoubtedly members of the Olds family were involved in séances. Wilbur and Sarah Sheets were the most prominent family members who participated. But clearly young Ransom had little interest or belief in the movement given his analytical and scientific mind.

Historical footnote: *A newspaper article from December, 1891 tells the story of a Professor Archer who came to Lansing from Middletown, Ohio to conduct séances. Admittance was $1 for men and 50 cents for women. According to the paper, the séance went well until the ghost of Ransom's grandmother was summoned. At that point, Ransom had had enough. 'He (Ransom) immediately went toward the cabinet and grasping the drapery of the spirit, held it high in the air and said "That is enough, I have the secret to your business" and pronounced the thing a fraud.' There was a great tussle between the participants and the medium's assistants and when the cabinet curtains were pulled back: they "behold the medium making great haste to clothe himself in the garb of humanity. At the time he appeared as a spirit, his outer garments had been entirely removed and it was in this deshabille he was found."*
Source: Lansing State Republican (1891)

The Pliny & Sarah Olds children:

Wilbur Jason Olds, born in 1850, was the oldest child of Pliny and Sarah Olds. Reportedly a Spiritualist, he spent much of his free time in the Cleveland area when the family lived there, attending meetings and séances. He was later described as a "neer do well, good but lacked purpose, fanatical" by Gladys Olds Anderson. Wilbur was reported to have left the family at age 14 to go west and was purportedly never heard from again. However, a recent discovery of family papers and public records now available on the Internet indicates an entirely different situation. Wilbur initially traveled with the family to Lansing in 1880. Wilbur married a local girl in Lansing in 1886 and then left her in Chicago just 6 weeks later. A small legal notice in a Chicago paper in 1886 referred to a court petition in which she wished to reclaim her maiden name. Wilbur married 2 more times and lived out his life in Los Angeles, California.

The recently discovered correspondence in the R.E. Olds papers at Michigan State University showed that R.E. supported Wilbur and his third wife for a number of years. Correspondence from Emory Olds, R.E. and Wilbur's brother indicates this arrangement was ongoing for several years until Wilbur died from uremia, Bright's disease and dementia in 1913.

Emory Whipple Olds born in 1853. Gladys Olds Anderson had previously commented to the author that Emory was insecure, not confident and had not been successful at various careers. He went through Business College at an early age. Emory had attempted a number of careers (traveling salesman, bookkeeper, and secretary/manager for R.E. personal affairs), most of them marginally successful, if successful at all. When R.E. left Olds Motor Works, Emory was sent several threatening letters by the Olds Motor Works Company management for a return of cars and payment of certain fees. Emory was quite upset in his letters to his brother and asking for help. Emory was to appeal to his brother numerous times for financial assistance. In one very poignant letter, he effusively thanks his brother for giving him a home and erasing all his debts. Emory married Charlotte Britton in 1875. They never had children. Emory last served as R.E.'s secretary and died of a heart attack while discussing business matters with his brother.

Wallace Samuel Olds, the third child, was born in 1856 and as a young man joined his father in the family engine business. He had excellent mechanical abilities like his father. In spite of a contentious period in their relationship when R.E. fired Wallace in 1898 for siding with the workers in a labor issue, Wallace was considered a good man and remained close to R.E. until his death in 1929. Gladys commented that Wallace was "gentle & good, very mechanical". Wallace and his wife were frequent guests on the Olds yachts over the years. Wallace ultimately ran a very successful machining business in Lansing.

Sarah Eliza Olds Sheets was the only daughter, born in 1859. She too was very close to R.E. over her life time. Gladys Olds Anderson commented that she had a "good intellect". Her husband, George, owned a men's clothing store in Grand Ledge. The Sheets, who had no children, traveled often with R.E. & Metta Olds. Sarah and George were apparently quite active in the Spiritualist community in Grand Ledge. George even owned the property where a local

Spiritualist camp operated. He also foreclosed on the camp when they couldn't pay their mortgage! The Sheet's home in Grand Ledge, which cost $19,000 in 1909 (a considerable sum in those days) was probably paid for by R.E. although no record exists today to support that assumption. The Sheets house later became the official residence for Michigan Governor Frank Fitzgerald for a period of time in the mid to late 1930's as well as home, at a later date, to the State's Supreme Court Justice. Governor Fitzgerald died in the home during his second term in March, 1939. Today it is known as the Sheets-Fitzgerald house and is privately owned.

LIST OF PHOTOGRAPHS AND ADVERTISEMENTS

		Page
1)	1883 advertisement for P. F. Olds & Son	3
2)	Olds first steam car (replica made by Joe Merli)	4
3)	1885 advertisement for Olds gasoline engine	5
4)	January, 1896 advertisement for Olds gasoline engine	6
5)	February, 1896 advertisement for Olds gasoline engine	6
6)	July, 1897 advertisement for Olds gasoline engine	7
7)	October, 1898 advertisement for Olds Gasoline Engine Works	7
8)	1892 Road Locomotive steam car (first US car exported)	8
9)	Reo Bird	10
10)	1896 drawing of Olds first gasoline engine car	11
11)	1897 Olds gasoline engine car (now at R.E. Olds Transportation Museum)	12
12)	1900 advertisement for Olds Marine Engines	14
13)	1900 advertisement for Olds Marine Engines	15
14)	1901 advertisement for Michigan Yacht & Power Company	16
15)	1905 advertisement for Olds Motor Works shares	20
16)	1905 Dirge for Leicester headline (1905 Glidden Tour)	22
17)	Rochester (sister ship)	23
18)	REOPASTIME	24
19)	REOMAR	27
20)	REOMAR: from Twentieth Century Engine Company brochure	28
21)	Twentieth Century Engine	28
22)	Aeolian Piano advertisement	30
23)	REOLA	32
24)	Launch at Elbamar	34
25)	Oldsmar, Florida marketing photograph	35
26)	1914 advertisement for REOMAR II – New York Yacht, Launch & Engine Co	38
27)	REOMAR II	38
28)	1912 "Farewell Car" advertisement	40
29)	Explosion of the REOMAR II	42
30)	Crew of REOMAR II	39
31)	REOLA II	44
32)	REOLA II docked at family home in Daytona Beach, FL	45
33)	REOLA II and REOMAR II docked together	46
34)	Lunch aboard the REOLA II	46

35) April 1923 advertisement for help on REOLA II..48
36) Elbamar advertisement...52
37) REOMAR III in Charlevoix...53
38) REOMAR III underway...54
39) REOMAR III engine room..55
40) Newspaper article of REOMAR III launching...56
41) Interior photo of REOMAR III...57
42) REOMAR III dining room..57
43) REOMAR III rear deck...58
44) REOMAR III stateroom..59
45) Olds family preparing to go ashore..60
46) Kohler ad for REOMAR III..61
47) Oldswood family cottage on Lake Charlevoix..62
48) REOMAR III in the 1990's..65
49) REOMETTA..67
50) REOMETTA interior..68
51) REOMETTA engine room..68
52) The Flying Cloud being delivered...70
53) The Flying Cloud underway...72
54) The Flying Cloud: before restoration and after..73
55) METTAMAR underway...74
56) Article with interior shots of METTAMAR...75
57) Article about REO diesel truck taking engine to METTAMAR.......................................76
58) METTAMAR engine..76
59) Photograph of family and friends on METTAMAR..78
60) METTAMAR being towed in Hudson, FL..80
61) REOMAR IV...81
62) REOMAR IV engine room..83
63) REOMAR IV underway...84
64) REOMAR IV lounge..85
65) Article on REOMAR IV saving two young boys..86
66) R.E. & Metta Olds on REOMAR IV at Perry's Monument, Lake Erie, Ohio................87
67) Article about Olds yacht REOMAR IV taken by US Navy for WWII effort..................87
68) REOMAR IV after conversion to USS ABILITY..89
69) Letter to R.E. Olds from Vice Admiral of US Navy..90
70) NAYADA...91
71) Captain Brow...92
72) METTAMAR II being launched..98
73) METTAMAR II underway..99
74) R.E. & Metta Olds aboard METTAMAR II...99
75) For sale brochure for METTAMAR II..100

76) Painting of REOLA III 101
77) REOLA IV 101
78) R.E. Olds in Matthews cruiser – Sealark 102
79) REOLA II 106
80) Oldsmar, Florida brochure 108
81) R.E. Olds preparing to swim 109
82) R.E. & Metta Olds in Chris Craft runabout – Oldswoode 110
83) Interior shot of METTAMAR 110
84) METTAMAR under construction 111
85) R.E. Olds and a group in a runabout 112
86) R.E. Olds driving his runabout – Oldswoode 112
87) Olds grandchildren being pulled by a yacht tender 113
88) REOMAR IV napkin 113
89) Laundry day on the REOMAR IV 114
90) Launch at Elbamar 114
91) Photograph of Olds boathouse on Round Lake, Charlevoix 115
92) Photograph of runabout Oldswoode, R.E. Olds in the stern 115
93) R.E. & Metta Olds at the family cottage in Charlevoix – Oldswood 116
94) R.E. Olds aboard the REOMAR IV 116
95) Early Olds launch 117
96) Gladys Olds (Anderson) 117
97) Launching runabout (2 photos) 118
98) R.E. Olds and Bernice Olds (Roe) 119
99) Expense ledger page – REOLA II 120
100) Launch – REOMAR II 121
101) REOMAR I 121
102) REOMAR II launch – shore party 122
103) REOMAR III swimmers 122
104) 1896 photograph – Olds first gasoline car 123

THE YACHTS OF R.E. OLDS

	Built Year	Name	Length (feet)	Beam (feet)	Draft (feet)	Engine	Designer	Builder	Where Built	Years Owned	Disposition
1	1907	Reopastime	54 ft. 6 in.	10 ft	2 ft. 3in	single 24hp; 4 cyl - gas	W. E. Collier	Racine Boat Manufacturing Co.	Muskegon, MI	1907 - 1909	Traded for bonds in 1910 to John H. Henderson
2	1909	Reomar	90 ft 9 in	14 ft 6 in.	3 ft.	2 - 30hp; gas	Cox & Stevens	NY Yacht, Launch & Engine Co.	Morris Heights, NY	1909 - 1911	traded for Reola - 1912
3	1912	Reola	60	13 ft. 8 in.	3	single 50hp; gas	Cox & Stevens	NY Yacht, Launch & Engine Co.	Morris Heights, NY	1912 - 1915	sold in 1915 to W. Bartley Henry
4	1912	Reomar II	98	16.3	4	twin 100hp - gas	Cox & Stevens	NY Yacht, Launch & Engine Co.	Morris Heights, NY	1912 - 1922	Traded for apartment building in Detroit
5	1914	Reola II	80	16	3 ft 2 in	twin 50hp	Cox & Stevens	NY Yacht, Launch & Engine Co.	Morris Heights, NY	1915 - 1923	sold 1923 to J.R. Wotherspoon
6	1924	Reomar III	100	18.7	4.6	twin diesels; 125hp each	Cox & Stevens	Defoe Boat & Motor Works	Bay City, MI	1924 - 1931	Traded for REOMAR IV (SYLVIA IV)
7	1926	Reomar IV	134	21.6	8	twin diesel; 300 hp each	Defoe Boat & Motor Works	Defoe Boat & Motor Works	Bay City, MI	1931 - 1942	Launched as the Sylvia IV; taken by the US Navy for use in WWII
8	1928	Reometta	63	15.5	6.3	twin 75hp diesel	NY Yacht, Launch & Engine Co.	NY Yacht, Launch & Engine Co.	Morris Heights, NY	1928	turned in after first run for Mettamar.
9	1928	Flying Cloud	38	8	2.6	single 150hp gas	Robinson	Robinson Marine Construction	Benton Harbor, MI	1928 - 1930	sold 1930
10	1928	Nayada	70	?	?	twin - 125hp gas	NY Yacht, Launch & Engine Co.	NY Yacht, Launch & Engine Co.	Morris Heights, NY	1939 - ?	Unknown
11	1930	Mettamar	93	19	4.6	twin - 125hp diesels	NY Yacht, Launch & Engine Co.	NY Yacht, Launch & Engine Co.	Morris Heights, NY	1930 - 1936	sold 1936
12	1948	Mettamar II	57	14.5	4	twin - 165hp diesel	Burger	Burger	Manitowoc, WI	1948 - 1949	sold 1949 - Jafco Marine Basin, Buffalo, NY
13	1949	Reola III	55	?	?	gas; hp unknown	Burger	Burger	Manitowoc, WI	1949 - 1950	traded for Reola IV
14	1950	Reola IV	58	14.7	4	gas; hp unknown	Burger	Burger	Manitowoc, WI	1950	sold after Olds' death
15	1937	Sealark	38	?	?	gas; hp unknown	Matthews	Matthews	Pt. Clinton, OH	? - 1951	sold after Olds' death

RUNABOUTS:
Oldswoode
Mettamora
Chieftain

Compiled by Peter J. Stephens & Gregory O. Stephens

CHAPTER ONE

THE EARLY YEARS
1880 TO 1903

"If you live your life with imagination and verve, God will play along just to see what outrageously entertaining thing you'll do next"

Dean Koontz

As a young boy, Ransom, or Ranny as he was called by the family (he preferred to be called R.E. in his adult years) was always tinkering with mechanical items. Perhaps in the beginning it was to get the attention of his father; Ranny was, after all, the youngest of 5 children; later as a young man he grew to just enjoy the challenges of handling machinery and solving problems. Once at a young age, he tried to rebuild an old watermill to help with his chore of keeping the house loaded with cut fire wood. His efforts to work on his watermill during a storm earned him a whipping from his father, but his tenacious nature soon earned his father's respect.

From the short family history presented earlier, one can see that life was difficult for the Olds family in those early days. Education was important but survival was a greater challenge. This was what might be considered a "working class" family today (there was no middle class back then). As the youngest, Ransom had many of the clean-up chores such as dealing with the horse, a story that would grow in legend as the reason why he was so focused upon mechanized or motorized carriages as a way to replace the horse. He would state numerous times over the years that the smell of a horse offended him. Young Ransom attended local Lansing schools and then attended the Lansing Business College in 1882 and 1883 where he learned the basics of accounting.

When the family relocated to Lansing in 1880, Pliny had just enough money to open a small machine repair shop on the west side of River Street, just south of Kalamazoo Street. R.E. was responsible for many of the basic chores around the shop. At that time Lansing did not have a city water works so Pliny and sons laid a hollow log under the street running from the shop to the Grand River. R.E. then operated a hand pump to pump water to the shop tank for the engine and boiler that ran the shop.

In 1883, Olds became a full time employee in his father's firm, P.F. Olds and Son. Interestingly, the "Son" in the company name was not Ransom but his brother, Wallace. Wallace, recently married and still living at home, was expecting a child and needed a home since he was living with his parents. A recently discovered draft of another R. E. Olds biography states that Wallace got into debt building a home for his wife and child so Pliny orchestrated a buyout of Wallace's interest by Ransom in 1885 for $1,100. While Wallace continued to work at the family business, he did not possess the drive of his younger brother to manage and control the destiny of the company.

Why or how Ransom was attracted to water and boating was never explained by him. Most likely it stems from the following experience with his first boat and the joy (plus money) it gave him to operate the boat on the open water versus the hot, grimy environment of a small factory and machine shop. It should be noted that building a boat would have been an expensive and difficult undertaking for a high school student, but clearly showed his work ethic and ingenuity. It was probably at this point that the joy of boating started to make an impact on the young Ransom.

R.E. was clearly an enterprising young man who was always on the lookout for a way to make some money. In 1882, R.E. built a 25' steam boat which was named the **MARY ANN** while still in high school. There is no family or public history to explain how a young man could build (or refurbish) a 25' boat without some type of lofting (design) experience or where the extensive woodworking experience that would be required came from. Nonetheless, in his written notes in the family archives, he states several times that he built the **MARY ANN**. According to the notes in a draft of his autobiography, Olds built the engine for the boat in his father's shop by creating a rudimentary steam engine. He used a spare small boiler and placed a gasoline burner under it. He then used the resulting steam to drive the boat's propeller. He offered Sunday afternoon cruises to local residents on Lansing's Grand & Red Cedar Rivers for a small fee. In Olds' words: it provided me "a good deal of extra pin money". No pictures exist today of the boat. We also have no clue as to how the name was selected.

After using the new propulsion system for his boat, Olds was approached by a man from Mason, Michigan who asked Olds to make one like it for him. R.E. agreed to make the engine for $100. The day before that engine was to be shipped, a man from St. John, Michigan said he thought there was a market for two or three engines in St. Johns and he offered to sell them. R.E. actually made six of his marine engines which the man successfully sold.

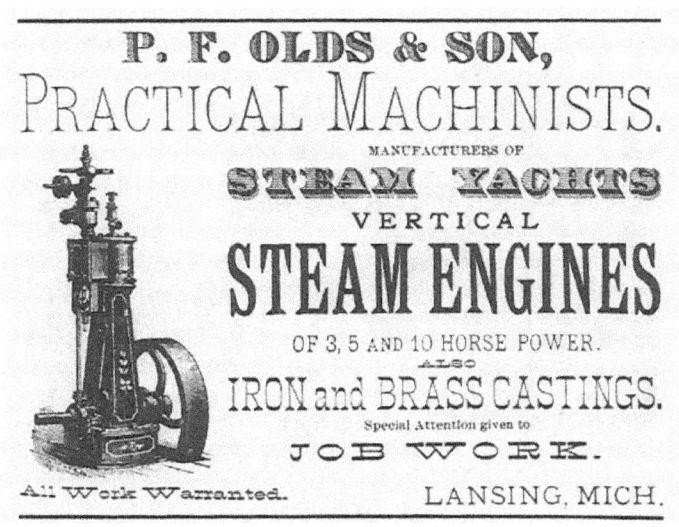

Source: Olds Family Archives – Stephens
1883 newspaper advertisement

As can be seen by the ad from 1883 when the P.F. Olds and Son firm was only three years old, the company already had targeted marine sales as a potential market. In 1883, P.F. Olds and Son entered into a contract to provide a steam engine for use in a boat capable of carrying up to a reported 100 passengers. Subsequently, the boat builder couldn't make the payment for the engine and defaulted on the contract. The Olds firm took possession of the boat as a result and young Ransom developed his first big entrepreneurial idea. In the words of R.E. Olds: "During the summer of 1886 & 1887, I ran a steam boat named *JUMBO* on the Grand and Red Cedar rivers. I made regular trips on holidays, Saturdays and Sundays. The fare was 25 cents for the round trip. Among my regular Sunday passengers were John Crotty, J. Edward Roe, James P. Edmonds and Maitland Buck." The profits from the boat were used to supplement the meager family income.

Clearly, R.E. was enjoying his time as a boater. At first, it probably met a financial need for the family but later became a source of joy and refuge from the hard work in his life. It also brought him his greatest joy, Metta, his wife. They married in 1889. According to great, granddaughter Clela Gray, "The weekend boat trip was where Grampa Olds met Metta. He thought she was beautiful." They met at the Waverly Park amusement park in Lansing, MI, which was one of the docking stops for the steamboat. The park lasted until 1917 when it closed. The *JUMBO* had been sold years before and has been lost to history.

At this time in Germany, in 1886, Karl Benz was granted a patent for his Patent Motorwagen, one of the world's first gasoline-powered cars. Simultaneously, R.E. was experimenting with his first steam car. Olds would continue to experiment with steam driven vehicles until 1896.

Source: R.E. Olds Transportation Museum
Joe Merli replica of Olds' first car

A year later than Benz, in 1887, Olds produced his first car, a 3 wheel steam vehicle. By Olds' own account, it was barely functional and extremely loud with gnashing, grinding gears. It produced one horsepower and so little torque so it was unable to overcome even slight rises in elevation. It also scared any horse within earshot during its solitary run on River Street in Lansing.

Meanwhile, business for the Olds firm was not good during the mid-1880's. Pliny had considerable difficulty making payrolls and eventually had to borrow money in 1885 from Robert Kedzie, a professor at Michigan Agricultural College. The Olds family business was now deeply in debt and on the edge of failing. Pliny was not considered to be a good businessman because he was too easy going and close to his workers. He typically was not strong nor stern enough to deal with employee issues. In contrast, R.E. had no problem dealing with employee issues or discord, including firing his brother, Wallace, for not staying aligned with the management of the family company during an employee strike.

R.E. started to have less time for boating at that time. At this point, as a partner in the family business, he was deeply concerned about the financial condition of the firm. This crisis made him aware of the negative impact of debt, but it was a lesson not fully learned until he later lost control of the family firm to Samuel Smith and his sons.

In 1886, in an effort to save P.F. Olds and Son, R.E. convinced his father to produce and advertise small gas or steam engines. Up to this point, according to Olds' autobiographical notes, P.F. Olds and Son was primarily a repair shop. R.E. felt the repair business was not a business that could be grown to any significant extent.

Source: Olds Family Archives – Stephens
1886 newspaper advertisement

Olds prevailed upon his father, who was an accomplished pattern maker to make some patterns for two or three sizes of engines. R.E. insisted on calling them gasoline engines but in fact they were gas fired steam boilers. It was an enormous gamble but one that paid off handsomely. P.F. Olds & Son Co. sold 2,000 small engines over several years thus allowing them to pay off their debts and achieve a solid financial base for the company. Interestingly, in another ad for P.F. Olds & Sons in 1886, they focused upon their Vertical Balanced Engines: "We build them from 3 to 60 horse-power, double and single, also with reverse motion for boats". Olds had also realized that marine applications were a potential market for them. In fact from this time well into the early 1900's marine engines were often more powerful and sophisticated than those found for automobiles. For many years, technological improvements in engines moved freely from marine to automotive and back again.

One wonders how a small machine shop employing less than a dozen people could build so many engines in such a short time period; perhaps R.E. was using early techniques of assembly line production that he would later develop for his automobile business? While we'll never definitively know, without Ransom's conviction to retire the business debt, there most likely would never have been the timely development of Olds' horseless carriage.

> Historical footnote: *According to the draft autobiography of Olds, his experience with the 6 marine engines gave him the idea to build similar engines for other applications. However, he soon discovered a flaw in his little engines: the boilers had a tendency to accumulate mud in the boiler when used for extended period of time thus resulting in a drop in power. But he found that when used for short periods of time, the accumulation of mud wasn't a problem. Olds, using his typical practical creativity set off on a letter writing campaign to country newspapers and butchers because he believed their power needs were sporadic and would be better sales candidates for this new small engine. The resulting sale of 2,000 engines between 1887 and 1892 saved the company and provided the financial and intellectual boost Olds needed to move on to his biggest project...a horseless carriage.*

Olds was feeling confident in his company and products. P.F. Olds & Son ran the following ads over the succeeding years as he continued to build the business.

Source: Olds Family Archives – Stephens

Source: Olds Family Archives – Stephens

The Farm Implement News   July 1897

Source: Olds Family Archives – Stephens

The Scientific American   October 15, 1898

Source: Olds Family Archives - Stephens

After the family firm was back on a solid financial footing, Olds and his father started expanding the gasoline engine works. The company continued to prosper through the 1890's. This change in fortune allowed Olds to continue his experimentation with steam driven vehicles. He built his second vehicle in 1892, which he called a "Road Locomotive", which was featured in Scientific American. Ultimately, the car was sold to the Francis Times Company, a London, England company with a branch office located in Bombay, India. This car became the first car exported from the United States. According to Olds expert the late Joe Merli, this may also have been the first front wheel drive vehicle! The two front wheels were powered by a fixed crank shaft that in turn was powered by two connecting rods that were powered by the steam engine, essentially a locomotive styled design. Unfortunately, the Road Locomotive had little torque and therefore could not climb hills. Also, there was a unique problem in that the locomotive could not stop once started! Interestingly, this car was made from the parts of Olds first steam car. The Road Locomotive's front wheels came from the rear wheels of the 3 wheeled steam car and parts for the new engine came from the first car's engine.

Source: Olds Family Archives – Stephens
1892 steam vehicle; first exported car from USA; R.E. Olds at the tiller

The factory had grown to 200 feet by 600 feet by 1899. The company which had been incorporated in July, 1890 was still called P. F. Olds & Son, Inc. Even the Panic of 1893, which caused considerable economic damage across the country, did not impact the Olds firm.

In 1893, Olds, with his wife and one year old daughter, visited the World's Columbian Exposition in Chicago. Here he purportedly saw an internal combustion gasoline engine. Interestingly, Henry Ford was also reputed to have attended the same fair and was impressed by the same exhibit. While no pictures of the exhibit exist today, it supposedly was a gasoline engine mounted on a work cart with its purpose being to pump water. As mentioned earlier, engines had already been developed for marine use, by Olds and other companies, but this exhibit prompted Olds and others to build internal combustion engines (soon called "hit and miss") for the horseless carriage concepts they were thinking about. Supposedly, Olds' new gas engines started selling better than his earlier gas fired steam boilers. In his later years, Olds also claimed to have seen a Benz gasoline and an electric self-propelled vehicles. He soon would be attempting to build both electric and gas cars. However it was clear to Olds, and others, that the drawbacks of steam (too long to prepare for driving) and electric (poor battery life) meant gasoline internal combustion engines would be the ultimate form of power for horseless carriages. But it would take the Detroit factory fire of 1901 to reaffirm his decision to move away from electric vehicles.

> Historical Footnote: *The Panic of 1893 caused a severe depression in the US that lasted until 1897. The cause of this panic started in Argentina with the failure of the 1890 wheat crop. European investors were concerned that this collapse would spread so they started a run on US gold reserves. At that time, one could cash US dollars in for gold. US wheat prices collapsed and railroad bankruptcies lead to a panic on the stock market and a run on the banks. Unemployment skyrocketed; in fact, Michigan's unemployment rate was an astonishing 43%! In 1896 Broadway had a play based upon the Panic called "The War of Wealth" about the disparity of wealth in the United States.*

Pliny F. Olds, in the early 1890's, had purchased a very small cottage on Pine Lake, now known as Lake Lansing. The cottage was located on a portion of the lake that had very shallow water. It should be noted that the lake was a popular gathering spot for Spiritualist meetings of the day, which Pliny and Sarah Olds regularly attended.

According to Olds' notes, R.E. conceived the idea of building a side wheel boat. There were two brothers on the lake that had a small boat shop and R.E. entered into a contract with them build this boat. Apparently boat building was not part of their normal skill set because R.E. found as they proceeded, the boat was poorly constructed. The brothers explained that if they weren't allowed to finish the contract, they could lose a substantial amount of money that would jeopardize their business. Undoubtedly, promises were made and assurances granted by the brothers that the vessel would be seaworthy upon completion. Olds found upon his first two trips across the lake that the boat leaked so badly that he decided to scuttle, or sink, the boat. On an early Sunday morning, he shoveled a great deal of sand into the boat and sank it in the deepest part of Lake Lansing.

This boat had been named the **LITTLE MAYFLOWER**. No pictures exist today of the boat. According to family records, the Olds family had several motorized boats at Lake Lansing; no pictures or descriptions of those boats survive except for the following 2 boats.

Source: Olds Family Archives – Stephens

In the early to mid 1890's, R.E. had an 18 foot launch named the **REO BIRD** (a name he would use again for a REO 32hp racing car driven by Danny Wurgis in 1905).

The **REO BIRD** was used by Olds for several years until it was replaced by the 20 foot **REO BIRD II**. Only a picture of the first **REO BIRD** exists today; the specifications, other than length, are lost. Olds would not have another boat until 1899 when he moved to Detroit as part of the expanded and recapitalized Olds Motor Works.

By 1896, using a carriage from the Clark & Company in Lansing, MI. Olds created his first vehicle with an internal combustion engine. This successful car, called the "Olds High Wheel Gasoline Motor Carriage" or a "vapor trap", resulted in the creation of the Olds Motor Vehicle Company in 1897 utilizing local Lansing, MI. investors.

In hind sight, Olds could not raise sufficient capital in Lansing to allow him to focus on the development of the horseless carriage. Further exacerbating his problems, was that he was trying to build the horseless carriages in a factory that was near or at full capacity. Olds simply didn't have the labor available to divert men to work on his motor vehicles. This obviously affected his production output but also had the effect of constraining his research and development of new prototype vehicles. Olds realized that he needed a separate and distinct facility if his motorized vehicles were going to sell. He also knew his family could not afford to take on a financial project of this magnitude.

Source: Olds Family Archives – Stephens
R.E. Olds, with the tiller, and Frank Clark (their wives are in the back)

Historical fact: Clark & Company, a large carriage maker and maker of the carriage in the above drawing, suffered from the Panic of 1893 and the ensuing economic depression which lasted until 1897. As a result, carriage making severely declined. Clark decided to build the Clarkmobile which only lasted from 1903 to 1904.

Historical Fact: *A Vapor Trap meant the engine drew its power from the vapor emanating from the gasoline. Trap refers to the body style in a carriage body wherein you could only get to the back seat by lifting the front seat up to enter; once in, the rear seat passenger was "trapped".*

The $50,000 capital raised by Lansing businessmen in 1897 for the new Olds Motor Vehicle Company was simply not enough. It allowed them the ability to continue development and build perhaps as much as six automobiles.

source: Smithsonian Institution
1897 Olds (now at the R.E. Olds Transportation Museum)

The 1897 Olds as described by the Smithsonian Institution: This vehicle was a four-wheel vehicle with solid rubber tires, a steering tiller and chain drive. Its six-horsepower, one cylinder, water cooled gasoline engine is under the body. The gasoline tank is suspended beneath the engine.

Olds would go through a series of financial restructurings for the next few years in an effort to raise sufficient funds to keep developing his horseless carriage prototypes. Four more gasoline vehicles were built in 1897 using the basic design from the 1896 model. A little known fact is that the 1896 also had the first built-in horn! The horn was activated with the use of the tiller. The one remaining 1897 gasoline vehicle now resides at the R.E. Olds Transportation Museum in Lansing, Michigan on loan from the Smithsonian Museum. This car, which carried four passengers, had a top speed of 10 miles per hour. The sole remaining 1899 Olds electric is also on display at the Olds Transportation Museum in Lansing, Michigan.

As "new" technology, it is easy to understand the difficulty Olds faced in obtaining financing for his motor vehicles. No one was willing to put large sums of money into an untested concept; that is, until Samuel L. Smith came along.

Olds recapitalized his companies, Olds Gas Engine Co. & Olds Motor Vehicle Co several times. Looking back, the financial restructurings were not done in sufficient size to provide long term growth and stability to Olds. It seemed that he was continually in discussion for financing which was clearly a distraction to him. It also slowed the rate of development and production, potentially putting him behind other fledgling car companies. However, it was clear that to seek additional capital for the Olds Motor Vehicle Co. (which was an unproven company) was a greater challenge since many did not share Olds' vision of the automotive future. Subscribers to the Olds Engine Works reorganization were plentiful due to the financial prosperity of that firm.

In reality, it took the sly and cagy Samuel L. Smith to offer a deal for a combined entity of both Olds companies. Olds had been to New York and Detroit, meeting with the leading financiers of the day but was uncomfortable with their offers for investing in the car company. The Olds Motor Works received a capital investment of $500,000 from Samuel Smith in 1899. Smith's deal gave Olds the money he needed and Smith got the security of the profits of the Olds Engine Company to protect his investment. The downside (to Olds personally) was the involvement of the Smith sons, Fred and Angus, who soon proved to be incompetent and would become the instigators of Olds' downfall.

The Smiths do deserve credit for providing the much needed capital to recapitalize the company as it grew its Olds Motor Works business but as a result, Olds lost voting control of his own firm. Pliny Olds had retired from the family company in 1894; there is no indication if the loss of control over the family firm caused any strife in the family. In fact, R.E. had moved his parents first to San Diego and then to Florida. He continued to support his parents in their retirement. His notes indicate a closeness with his father. There is a letter from Pliny in 1905 in the family archives wherein Pliny is admonishing R.E. to slow down or risk hurting his health.

Between 1897 and 1899, Olds also had designed and produced 4 Stanhope electric vehicles: one runabout, several light delivery vehicles and a four seat Cabriolet. Per Wikipedia:
"A Stanhope is an archaic car body style characterized by its single bench seat mounted at the center, folding cloth top, and a dashboard at the front. All Stanhopes featured tiller steering, either in the center or at the side."

All of these vehicles were electric powered. With over half of the existing 8,000 automobiles in the USA being electric at that time, Olds thought his electric autos would get immediate acceptance in the city environment of that era because they were clean (no smoke), quiet (no backfire), ready to go and didn't involve any gear shifting. Steam cars took from a half to full hour to prepare and required more mechanical knowledge to handle. Internal combustion cars, which required hand cranking, still scared people with the thought of an explosion to power the car. So electrics were pursued by Olds and others for primarily city use. Olds was soon to see that internal combustion cars with their larger gasoline tanks and ease of refilling would soon become the preferred motive power due to the larger distances that could be traveled. Later, the early internal combustion engines were used primarily in the cities, a push soon arose to upgrade roads so that cars could travel easily and quickly between cities or take day trips to the country.

From 1899 to 1902, the Olds family lived in Detroit where he could be in charge of production at the Detroit manufacturing facility. S. L. Smith required Olds' move to Detroit where he thought more labor and raw materials would be available and Olds could be more creative in his designs. In addition to electric powering generators and city lighting, Detroit's infrastructure offered an easy way to recharge the electric cars. It is interesting to note that Olds started the development of his assembly line at this point using **sawhorses on wheels** so workers could use their assigned parts in the construction of an automobile. Some parts still required finished machining.

After moving to Detroit in 1899, Olds was offered the opportunity to purchase a 35 foot cruiser named the ***EAST WIND***. According to Olds, he used this boat for two seasons. While no picture exists today of the cruiser, we know from the August 12, 1900 newspaper ad below that it must have been quite a vessel for its day. With a 6 hp Olds gasoline engine, it also came equipped with a folding lavatory and a water closet. Notably it was "especially adapted for hunting and fishing…"

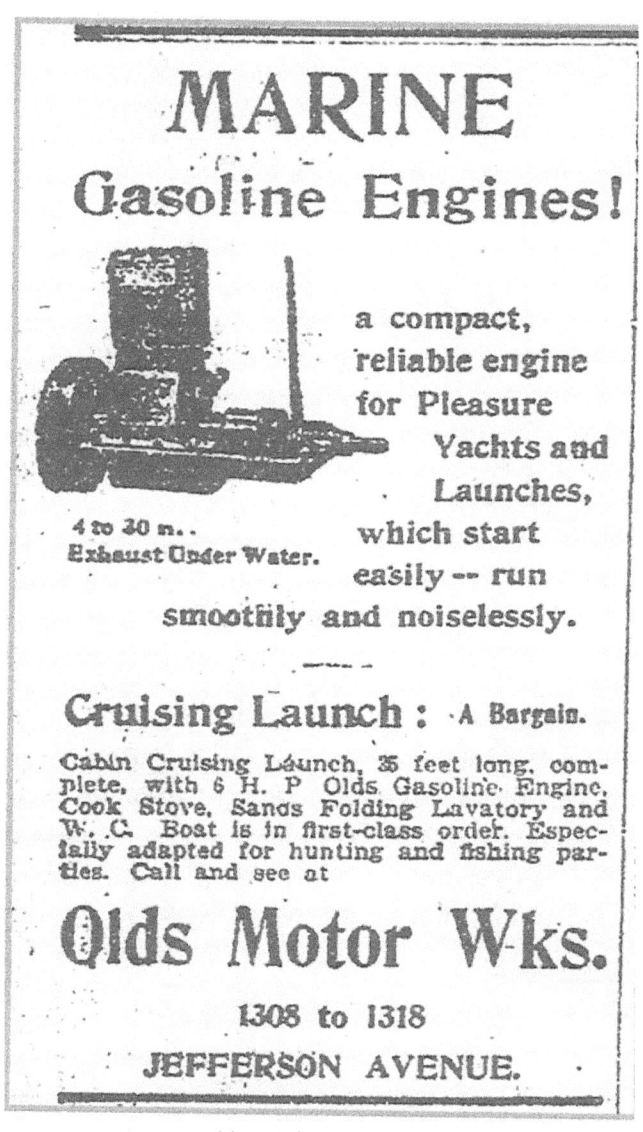

Source: Olds Family Archives – Stephens
August 12, 1900

In early 1900, Olds had purchased the marine engine business of Charles Brady King. King was a very notable figure in the early automotive days. King built and drove the first car in Detroit in March of 1896, with Henry Ford riding a bicycle behind him. The marine engine business was purchased to further increase the profits of the Olds Gasoline Engine Works which Smith felt would protect his investment In Olds Motor Works. King was retained to run the marine engine division for Olds as Chief Engineer. The following ad ran in March, 1900 shortly after the purchase of King's marine engine business.

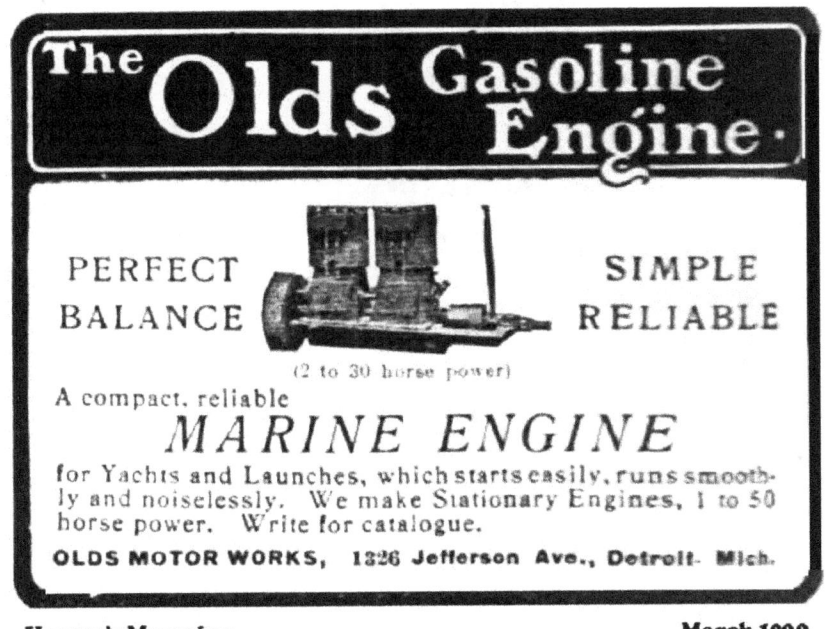

Source: Olds Family Archives - Stephens

Unfortunately a fire occurred on March 9, 1901 that destroyed the Olds plant, arguably the only plant dedicated to automobile production in Michigan and perhaps the USA. The fire that destroyed the Detroit plant of Olds Motor Works subsequently forced the sale of the Olds Marine Division back to King and a partner in the latter part of 1901. King then joined with Michigan Yacht and Power Co. This sale was necessary in order to raise funds and refocus the Olds Company on automobile production.

Source: Olds Family Archives - Stephens

The above ad was run shortly after the sale of the Olds Marine Division to Michigan Yacht & Power Company.

> *Historical fact:* Michigan Yacht and Power was formed in 1890. The company manufactured small power boats and were distributors of marine engines, including Olds engines. In 1901, Michigan Yacht and Power purchased both the Sintz Gas Engine Company and the Olds Marine Division. Interestingly, a Sintz engine was used in 1894 in a Haynes car. Haynes later formed a company to produce Haynes Apperson cars. Sintz also built a gasoline engine car in 1897 but the company never went any further. When one of the original partners of Michigan Yacht and Power sold his interest in 1905, the company was renamed Gray Marine Motor Company, a name well known to boaters of the day and now to classic boaters of today.

Following the Smith's insistence towards larger vehicles, Olds had developed approximately a dozen different models. Prices ranged from $1,200 for a small two person trap to nearly $3,000 for a four person trap. These models, while mostly gas, included a few electric models.

Olds had realized that the large gas and electric models were not popular and not selling because they were too complicated and unreliable. Due to the growing financial losses of the firm, Olds, his senior engineer and his test driver decide to build a small one cylinder vehicle. Olds was now refocused on his original vision of a small reliable automobile, much to the annoyance of the Smiths. The small car was road tested in November, 1900 on Belle Isle, just over the bridge from the factory. Three more test models were built and road tested during the winter of 1900/1901. The company approved the final design in February, 1901 and a preliminary sales catalog was created and distributed. Nearly 350 orders were received for this new smaller car prior to the fire.

It was believed that up to 15 experimental vehicles, including electric and gasoline, were made just prior to the 1901 Olds plant fire. The Olds Motor Works accountant, Theodore Barthel, stated in the 1950's that 2 electrics, 9 Curved Dash, 2 traps and 1 dismantled Curved Dash were destroyed in the fire. The Olds auto business had been losing significant money to that point ($80,000 annual loss) and Olds was under great pressure from the Smiths to get the business turned around and generate profits.

Later, investigators determined that the natural gas connection had a leak that ignited. The resulting fire burst a 3 inch gas main which accelerated the fire and explained why the buildings burned so fast. After the fire, they discovered structural integrity issues in the first building. 14 inch thick brick walls on the first story narrow considerably going into the upper floors which may have contributed to the amount of destruction.

One of the great legends from the fire was that all the plans as well as models for the cars intended to be sold were destroyed in the fire leaving only the Curved Dash prototype (CDO) to be taken apart for patterns. Late in the evening of March 10, Olds stated to the local newspaper that his chief draftsman told him all the drawings and plans for all cars were found in the company vault. In addition to the timekeeper, James Brady, pushing the CDO out the front door, the accountant, Theodore Barthel, carried the account books out as well.

The question of whether or not the plans for the electric cars were lost or not is a debatable academic issue. Olds himself stated the plans were undamaged in the fire. According to George May's book, *R.E. Olds, Auto Industry Pioneer*, the advance orders for the Curved Dash probably doomed the electric car anyway, not to mention the continuing issues with the batteries of the day. In any event, the fire forced Olds to increase outsourcing his parts to companies that were also emboldened to consider building their own horseless carriages. This outsourcing became the industry standard as did Olds' requirement that the factory be paid in full for all cars shipped to the sales agencies. (A number of companies felt Olds would never recover from this disaster, and rushed into production trying to take advantage of the situation). Even his factory neighbor, Will Barbour of Detroit Stove Works, came out with the Northern runabout in 1902. Even the manager of the Olds Automobile Department left to manufacture and sell his own car, the Murray runabout. The vehicle was a shameless copy of the Curved Dash.

In a letter from Charles Hulse, an automotive historian in the 1950's, he quotes Fred Smith, former VP at Olds Motor Works, as saying, at the time of the fire, they had a number of electric cars but no waiting customers. Many years later, Smith thought they may have sold one or two of the electrics.

An interesting side note of the decision to make the Curved Dash the key model prototype for the company is that the rest of the world was focused primarily upon building larger cars for the wealthy. The assumption was that automobiling, like horses, would be a thing of the wealthy. Only the wealthy could afford the chauffeur or stable man. Because Olds established the small affordable car as the future of the industry, it solidified Michigan as the center of the automobile industry which produced low priced cars at a very high volume versus other states with factories that produced lower volumes but much higher priced cars.

The reality of the situation is that Olds had been indecisive about the various larger models he had been developing. None of them sold well and Olds himself still liked the idea of small cars which he was now starting to see be built in small numbers in other factories. So the realization of poor sales for the larger models, practical and technical issues with steam engines and electric batteries plus the awareness that smaller cars price point might indeed be within the reach of more people, led Olds to conclude his Curved Dash runabout was the solution to his company's problems. In fact his order book was reputed to be 350 orders for the runabout with much fewer order for the electrics. The March, 1901 fire just accelerated his decision.

The Curved Dash succeeded in meeting Olds' requirement for a simple, easy to use and inexpensive machine. He hoped this might finally be the answer to stopping the losses the company was experiencing. Approximately 425 Curved Dash Olds were built in 1901 after the fire. Even the factory fire couldn't slow down the production of the world's first mass produced car because nearly every part was being supplied under contract by outside suppliers.

It is well known that these were difficult times for Olds as he increasingly battled the Smiths over key questions of product design and management. Olds himself was hospitalized in 1901 for several months due to a chronic but unnamed illness. According to the family files, Olds could see the factory and the test cars from his hospital window which must have added considerable angst to his life since he was unable to have any input into the operations during his hospitalization.

By 1903, Olds was exceedingly frustrated by the attempts of the Smith brothers to micro manage and change the focus of the company away from small affordable cars. The Smiths, who wanted gasoline engines over electric, were pushing hard for larger, luxurious vehicles that catered to the wealthy. Olds envisioned a world where the general population could easily afford a mass produced and inexpensive car. While not directly articulated, Olds was essentially talking about a "Middle Class" which hadn't developed yet. Olds' feeling on this societal change would reappear later with his Oldsmar, Florida project. The Smiths were not without their justified concerns: most people could not afford a car at any price, their company had quality issues and new car development seemed slow and unfocused. By the end of 1903, R.E. left the company he created when he was removed as an officer of the company at its annual meeting. He was exhausted and tired of fighting. He received a $1,000,000 in stock (worth nearly $27,000,000 in 2018 dollars) and a "promise" to help him sell it in the market. He was a very wealthy man and only 40 years old. The Smiths then embarked upon a perverse campaign to drive down the share price in order to repurchase the shares!

> **Historical fact**: *the Smiths had to sell the Olds Motor Vehicle Company to Durant in 1908 to save some portion of their original investment. Their insistence on building large cars for the wealthy had proven to be disastrous. Compounding this poor judgment, the Smith's also invested in Owen Motor Car Company to produce another big and powerful car with a 60-hp motor, 42 inch wheels, and a 120-inch wheelbase. The touring model was priced at $3,250 and a closed body was $4,800. Further, in an ironic twist of fate, Olds, through The REO Motor Car Company, purchased the Owen Motor Car Company when it was in financial straits, purportedly for a patent for a special center control steering mechanism. The investors, including the Smith Brothers, were able to retrieve a portion of their investment by receiving REO stock. Olds had consistently proved the Smith's wrong about the automobile market and the Smith's managerial ineptitude had cost them millions personally.*

The seeds of R.E. Olds' yachting enthusiasm had been established at an early age. Initially, "being on the water" was a source of income but, later, as his life and health became much more complicated with the growing automotive challenges, he found solitude and, most importantly, quality time with his family starting with his first cruiser in Detroit. Olds was to go on to invent many other products and create numerous other companies over the next decade. He was a man of considerable energy and vision. While he would become energized by a mechanical or logistical problems; once he invented a devise or solution or created a new business, he would quickly move on to another venture. He was a "serial" entrepreneur in the truest sense! He certainly was not an administrator; day to day business issues bored him. He wanted to do big, bold projects. Over the next decade, a pattern soon emerged. He sought to balance his frenetic business life with an almost equally active social life. Yachting was soon to play a major role in determining that balance.

> **Bonus historical facts**:
> *(i) Metta Olds often accompanied her husband on his early morning test drives with his first cars. In fact, Metta was an integral part of supporting R.E.'s efforts at developing his cars. In 1894, Olds made his first automobile trip to Grand Ledge. In his words: "This was in a high wheeled car with 1 ½ inch solid rubber tires." (Author note: Olds comments that the car is similar to the one in the Smithsonian Institution, which is now at the R.E. Olds Transportation Museum in Lansing, Michigan). Olds continues: "It was a real feat to get this car up the so-called "Big Hill" on Saginaw Road. My wife followed behind the car with a large stick of wood, so as to prevent the car from rolling back down the hill if it stopped."*
> *(ii) In June, 1944 at the luncheon at the Hotel Olds, held by the Rotary Club, for Olds' 80th birthday, Olds told the story of one of his early Curved Dash cars that would only carry men. As soon as a woman got in, "the car would stall and refuse to budge". Olds analytically determined that the cause was when the full skirts of the "fair passengers pressed against a flap attached to the cushions, causing a short circuit in the coils under the seat". Charles Nash, Chairman of the Nash-Kelvinator Corp. then said to Olds in response: "You were then also the inventor of the first automatic car parker."*

Aut inveniam viam aut faciam
"I shall either find a way or make one"

CHAPTER TWO

THE GLORY YEARS
1904 TO 1920

If you can't wait for your ship to come in, you've got to row out to it!
Greer Garson

1904 started with R.E. Olds being out of a job for the first time since his high school days. He was a rich man, in stock, not cash. He also wanted to liquidate his Olds Motor Works stock as holding it might imply a continuing support for the Smith management with whom he vehemently disagreed. Olds was hoping for $30 dollars a share but soon found that the Smiths tried to manipulate the stock price and drive it lower in an effort to strike back at Olds. To escape, Olds took a long vacation to San Diego, California with his family to regroup after the fallout with the Smiths. The family went by rail and added numerous side trips to entertain their 2 young daughters, Gladys & Bernice. After visiting with his parents, Pliny and Sarah, the family headed back to Lansing and a financially secure but uncertain future.

Courtesy Detroit Free Press, February 16, 1905

During this time period of the family vacation, there are numerous ads in national periodicals offering the sale of blocks of Olds stock. Olds had been in continual contact with the Delano Co. but also had several other brokerage firms peddling Olds' shares and they all were struggling to offset the Smith's negative news. It seems perverse for the Smith's to overtly drive down the share price of the company they invested in but that, in fact, was their plan.

Upon his return, Olds was approached by numerous friends who, in his absence but probably with his concurrence, put together a consortium of investors to fund a new automobile company. Interestingly, it seems that Olds initially was wanted as a figurehead for the new car company; an early example of 'branding'. A letter from R.M. Owen dated December 9th, 1904 states "As we have explained before, the only reason we wish to have your name connected with this corporation was for advertising reasons." He was, after all known as the "Father of the American Automobile Industry" as declared by his peers.

Eventually he was convinced or, more likely, decided that his personal involvement was required. It was his nature to be initially totally hands-on with his projects. Certainly, one might imagine a tad of spitefulness in his decision to get re-involved in the automobile industry although Olds never reacted publically in that manner. Indeed many years later, after Olds published a memoir in 1949 called **"Auto Pioneering"**, he received a letter from Fred Smith, the son of Samuel Smith, excoriating him on what Smith deemed a "fanciful" account of the early days of Olds Motor Works. Olds responded simply with "you and I should be glad that we live in a country where, and in a period when, a man can express his thoughts freely".

After Olds agreed to the terms of the new automobile venture in which he retained 51% controlling interest, men were hired and placed in facilities around Lansing, Michigan to avoid detection by the Smiths. These engineers were designing the first REO. The new company was announced on August 17, 1904. By October 15th, R.E. Olds started the first test run of the new REO which would eventually total 2,000 miles. The first REO's were shipped on March, 1905.

Over the course of 1904 and 1905, R.E. Olds was an incredibly busy man. In addition to starting REO Motor Car Company, he had his home on 720 South Washington St. in Lansing built for $25,000. He was awarded 5 patents, acquired Bancroft Peat Fuel & Cement Co., acquired the Hollister Building in downtown Lansing, served as President of the Correspondence School of Automobile Engineering (later absorbed by the New School of Automobile Engineers), devised and ordered the design & construction of the Baby REO (the world's first fully functional miniature car), and he still had the REO Company to run! Olds also, for good measure, became the Chairman of a pipe organ company; one suspects that this was done because of: a) his love of music and b) he had just installed a large pipe organ in his new home in Lansing.

Olds was traveling a great deal to promote his new car company. He devised a number of creative marketing ideas that ultimately solidified his standing as one of the earliest and greatest automotive marketers. 1905 was a busy year for Olds and his multitude of marketing ideas. The first ever double transcontinental trip was done by Percy Margargel & David Fassett. Margargel's car, in fact, was the first camper in America: it was outfitted with a windlass, cable and a Pullman sleeper. Anna Andrews, the driver of a REO, was one of 4 cars that finished the Chicago to St. Paul Endurance Run. She later became the first female Reo dealer. The REO Bird, a 32 hp racing vehicle driven by Danny Wurgis, was winning multiple events during the year. Olds himself drove a REO 5 passenger touring car in the 1905 Glidden Tour. You may see footage of this tour on YouTube® (search: First Glidden Tour 1905). The REO (with R.E. Olds driving) is at minute 4:09 & 5:43.

> **DIRGE FOR LEICESTER.**
>
> Automobolists Draped Machines Where Drivers Had Been Fined.

Courtesy Washington Post, Jul 22, 1905

> **Historical fact**: *There is a wonderful story about Olds and the other Glidden race participants being stopped in Leicester, Mass for speeding at the appalling speed of 15mph! The judge, who was no fan of the newfangled automobile, severely chastised the automobilists for their careless and dangerous behavior. Each of them was fined $15. Olds then proceeded to hire a band to lead them out of town. The band and cars were festooned in black mourning bunting. The band was instructed to play a funeral dirge as the band and cars proceeded (slowly) out of town. As soon as the party hit the town limits, they resumed their normal high speed of 15 to 20 mph until they reached their next destination.*

1906 started with a huge marketing sensation. The Baby REO car was introduced at the New York Auto Show to wide acclaim. The company was inundated with orders for the miniature car. In fact, there were more orders for the small car than its full sized companion, the REO Model A. The little car embarked upon a national tour making stops at REO dealers, car shows, children's hospitals and any other venue that might bring attention to the new REO Company. After a remarkable "life", including being lost several times, the Baby REO (and its full sized Mama) are on display at the R.E. Olds Transportation Museum in Lansing, Michigan. (Disclosure: The Mama and Baby REO are owned by the author and his wife).

Also during 1906, Olds founded 4 more companies: National Coil Co., Atlas Drop Forge Co., Capital National Bank (Lansing, MI.) and Michigan Screw Co.

By the end of 1906, Olds must have been ready for a rest. Remembering his early days on the water, Olds chartered a houseboat in the winter of 1906 called the "***ROCHESTER***". According to Olds' notes, it had six bedrooms.

This photo, while not of the **ROCHESTER**, shows a similar style of "houseboat" for that era.

(The Rudder, December, 1906: Vol XVII, No. XII)

The Olds invited five other couples to join them and they took it down the Inland Waterway from Jacksonville to Miami and the Florida Keys. As was to become his custom, he loved surrounding himself with a large number of family and guests. According to his daughter, Gladys Olds Anderson, it was such an enjoyable excursion for the 12 travelers that Olds commissioned the building of the yacht "**REOPASTIME**" upon his return home.

The First Yacht: The REOPASTIME built in 1907; owned by Olds from 1907 to 1909

The **REOPASTIME** would be considered a power sail craft back in the day but the sails were rarely used. Olds' subsequent yachts would be motor yachts, occasionally accented by sailing masts. "He didn't have the patience for sailboats. They were too slow." according to his daughter, Gladys Olds Anderson.

Source: Olds Family Archives – Ed Roe

REOPASTIME was a wooden day motor cruiser of a trunk cabin style designed by W.E. Collier and built by the Racine Boat Building Company of Muskegon, Michigan in 1907. Her LOA (length overall) was 54 feet 6 inches with a 10 foot beam (width). The yacht was a single screw powered by a single 24 horsepower, 4 cycle, 4 cylinder, Racine motor. It was a shallow draft boat appropriate for Florida waters. The yacht drew only 2 feet, 3 inches. The fantail or flush deck stern was suitable for outdoor seating with a canvas sunshield to protect the guests. The yacht carried 2 lifeboats which was probably not enough for the number of passengers and crew the **REOPASTIME** was usually carrying. More likely given the absence of safe boating regulations at that time, the dinghies were reserved for transporting guests to shore for day excursions or evening accommodations. This size motor vessel could easily be handled by the captain and a crew of 2 mates.

The State Republican newspaper, forerunner of the Lansing State Journal, described the **REOPASTIME** in an article, entitled "**R.E. Olds Goes South**" in the January 12, 1907 edition: *"The REOPASTIME is one of the most modern and up-to-date private yachts afloat and can* *accommodate 10 passengers besides the crew. Supplies for a month can be carried...Being equipped with electric lights, baths and other modern improvement, passengers have all the conveniences to which they are accustomed to on land. The cabins are all furnished in mahogany with white enameled paneled ceilings. Besides an Estey organ, several other musical instruments are provided for the entertainment of the passengers. On the upper deck are kept the power tender and rowboats. In addition to the upper deck, the yacht has a 10-by-10 foot afterdeck."*

Historical fact: *Estey Organs were the largest organ makers in the world. The company began in 1852 and lasted until 1961. Over 500,000 pump reed organs and 3,000 pipe organs were made by the company. The company also made over 160 theatre organs during the silent film era. After World War II, Estey became an innovator in the new field of electronic organs. Changing music interests and foreign competition caused the company to cease operations in 1961.*

In order to get the yacht to Florida, Olds had to locate a flatbed railroad circus car which was the only practical way to get the yacht from Northern Michigan to Florida. According to his daughter, Gladys, Olds found the necessary flatbed circus car in St. Louis, Mo. He leased it and had it sent to Muskegon, Michigan where it picked up the **REOPASTIME** and took it to Palatka, Florida. However, it had to be routed so there were no tunnels!

The helm was located atop the salon and next to the foremast. This helm was exposed to the elements. It is not known if there was a lower inside helm although photographs of crew in the front salon windows suggest in fact that may have been a lower enclosed helm. Most yachts of this style did in fact have an inside helm. In other photographs, the windows for that front salon are closed suggesting an area the Olds wished to keep out of view.

The purpose of this yacht was day cruising so accommodations and galley/kitchen space was minimal. There was a large protected salon space for guests in case of a sudden Florida storm.

Historical fact: *In 1908, R.E. Olds wanted a car for his use in Florida while cruising on the **REOPASTIME**. According to his daughter, Gladys, she noted in her journal that R.E. had a REO sent by railroad to Jacksonville, Fl. There he had it loaded on to a boat to be sent down the St. John's River to Sanford, Fl. The trip took from 3pm to 11am the following day. When it arrived, the crew unloaded it on the east bank of the river slightly east of Sanford. Thereupon, it headed for Deland and ultimately Daytona Beach by following the "Pine Needle Highway".*

For the uninitiated, there were few roads in the early 1900's in Florida. Roads were cut through pine thickets and the stumps were left as an indication of the route. In 1912, it was noted that there were signs every 25 miles or so declaring that one was still on the road. There was great risk of being lost in the Pine Barrens. The reason it was called a Pine Needle Highway is because pine needles were used to neutralize the sand. In some areas, the sand was so soft as to make the road impassable and the "quicksand" presented grave dangers to travelers. So pine needles, moss or dried vegetation was used to firm up the road. The sand on one road showed such "unbelievable depth and softness" that it required a ton of pine needles per mile to make the road passable.

In the April 18, 1912 issue of "The Automobile", a full 4 years after R.E. drove his car from Sanford to Daytona Beach, declared "Florida emphatically is not a field for touring at present". The magazine also

> *declared "in some ways, Florida is wilder and rougher as a touring ground than any state east of the Mississippi River..."*

The yacht was used during their winter months' vacation and was moored at the family estate on Halifax Avenue in Daytona Beach, which had been acquired in 1906. The **REOPASTIME** was used for 3 years until it was sold late in 1909. The **REOPASTIME** was R.E's reentry into yachting, a pursuit he would continue up until his death.

The **REOPASTIME** was traded for an unspecified number of bonds. The purchaser was John H. Henderson from Pittsburgh, PA. Mr. Henderson was a Superior court Judge in Pittsburgh. After the Henderson ownership, the fate of the **REOPASTIME** is unknown.

REOMAR: built in 1909; owned by Olds from 1909 to 1911

Olds had clearly "gotten the bug". He wanted now to go beyond short range day cruises and have the option to cruise comfortably for longer distances. He also wanted the finer amenities that his wife, family and guests expected.

The car business was doing exceedingly well. Olds had once again established himself as one of the leaders of the industry. In 1909, REO Car Company produced 6,592 cars up from 864 cars in his first year of production in 1905. In fact, demand for his cars, which were deemed well-built and solid, far exceeded production in future years. Olds was extremely concerned about quality, no doubt a lingering feeling from the Olds Motor Works days. He sometimes restricted production much to the consternation of the sales force. If the raw material or specific part did not meet his standards, he would reduce production until the problem was solved. In 1911, rear axle problems resulted in a 21.7% drop in revenue from reduced production. In fact, there has been speculation that Olds did not have the drive or ambition of a Henry Ford and he was content to allow his company to grow slowly. There certainly is some empirical evidence to support this assertion. Olds claimed for the second time that he controlled nearly 25% of the US automobile market and was a major exporter of cars, yet he let his company lose its market share over the ensuing years.

Source: Olds Family Archives - Stephens

His next yacht was the **REOMAR** which was designed by the well-known naval architecture firm of Cox & Stevens of New York City. The **REOMAR** was built in 1908 and launched in 1909. The yacht was manufactured by The New York Yacht, Launch and Engine Company at Morris Heights, New York City. The design is a wooden trunk cabin cruising motor yacht designed for southern waters. Its length was 90 feet, 9 inches with a beam of 14 feet, 6 inches. Along with a high freeboard, it had a shallow draft of 3 feet more commonly found on southern cruising yachts; it also was designed to be well ventilated due to the southern humidity.

The following images were taken from the 1910 catalog for Twentieth Century Engine Company.

YACHT "REOMAR"
90 feet x 15 feet. Two 30-h. p. 20th Century Motors. Owned by R. E. Olds, Lansing, Mich.

Source: Olds Family Archives - Stephens

Source: Olds Family Archives - Stephens

The yacht was powered by twin 30 horsepower, Twentieth Century engines, 6 ½ inch stroke X 8 ½ bore, with bronze propellers of 30 inches each. The cruising speed was 11 or 12 miles per hour or roughly 10.5 knots. Fuel was supplied by twin gasoline tanks holding a total of 350 gallons. The gasoline tanks were designed to be seamless to lower the risk of leaking and fire.

Interestingly, the yacht with its balanced stern and bow, twin pole masts, engine stack and deckhouse was intentionally designed to look like a steamer yacht. **REOMAR** required a crew of 4 in addition to the captain.

The keel and frames were made of white oak, yellow pine for the planking, white pine for the decks and mahogany for the trunk cabin, deckhouse, and interior joinery. Electric lighting was provided by separate gasoline engines. The yacht also carried 1,200 square feet of sail. The sails and rigging were designed to be sufficient to handle the yacht in the event of a mechanical breakdown.

The dining room was forward of the bridge which was finished in specially selected solid mahogany. The dining table seated 12 people. There was also a mahogany sideboard. The galley and engine adjoined the dining room. The crew quarters were finished in oak and had sleeping accommodations for 5 crew members.

R.E. and Metta Olds' quarters were located just aft, or behind, the space for the engine compartment. There were 2 large double beds along with bureaus and wardrobes. Everything was finished in mahogany. There were additional accommodations on board: 1 single stateroom portside with a 40 inch berth with drawers underneath, a bureau and a folding seat; across from that room was a bathroom with a porcelain tub and fixtures. All plumbing fixtures allowed for hot and cold running water. Forward of the stateroom and bathroom were two large staterooms each with double-width bunks, bureaus, wardrobes for hanging clothes as well as folding wash basins. There were sleeping accommodations for 10 guests.

The salon/saloon was 12 by 11 feet and contained an Aeolian automatic piano (see ad below). The salon also had a writing desk and a lounging sofa that wrapped around the aft end of the salon and stern. These sofas were wide enough to be available for berths. The entire cabin was constructed of solid mahogany. The after deck had trunk storage under it for the steamer trunks when they were unpacked.

Source: Olds Family Archives - Stephens

> Historical fact: Aeolian Organ & Music Co. produced automatic organs and pianos. Interestingly, their main market was towards the wealthy not the church market. The profit margins from the manufacturing and installation of upscale residential pianos and chamber organs were significantly higher than the highly competitive and thus lower margin, church segment.

Olds was quoted in the *Lansing Journal*, May 16, 1909, that "his plan is to entertain at different times, about 30 friends during the coming summer". The trip of summer 1909 was to leave New York, travel down the Long Island Sound to Narragansett and return up the Hudson River to Albany, then through The Champlain canal to Lake Champlain to the Richelieu River canal to the St. Lawrence River. After that, the Olds family visited Quebec, Montreal, Kingston and the Thousand Islands where they remained for several weeks.

In 1910, R.E. and Metta Olds plus a group of friends arrived in Daytona to visit his mother who was living in Seabreeze, an area of Daytona now incorporated into Daytona Beach. The local paper announced their arrival and that the **REOMAR** *"is one of the handsomest ever brought to these waters"*. The yacht was soon to leave to cruise the Keys with even more guests coming aboard.

REOMAR was used primarily in Florida for 2 years and then traded in for the **REOLA**, the next in the series of the Olds yachts. Cox & Stevens was listed as the transfer agent and handled the sale of the yacht **REOMAR** to a N. L. Carpenter of New York in February, 1911. The **REOMAR** was then renamed the **NATCHEZ**. In February, 1913, the **NATCHEZ** is listed as being sold to Commodore Dowse, President of Reed & Barton Co., a well-known maker of silverware. Under ownership of Commodore Dowse, the **NATCHEZ** was renamed the **DORMARBEA**. Under command of Captain Allen of St Augustine, Florida, the yacht was frequently brought down from the north through the "inside channel", now called the Intercostal Waterway.

According to Power Boating magazine, the **DORMARBEA** was sold in 1914 to Thomas Roberts Jr. of Philadelphia, who renamed the yacht the **KILKENNY**, and later sold it in 1917 to Edward Crozier, also of Philadelphia.

The **KILKENNY** had an interesting history for the next quarter century. First, Jesse Livermore, an early Wall Street speculator who made and lost several fortunes in his life before committing suicide in 1940 at the age of 63, was an interested buyer. As described in the February 17, 1917 edition of the Wilmington, Delaware, *The News Journal* newspaper, Livermore was on his way to see and possibly negotiate for the purchase of the **KILKENNY**. However, all the "upper" berths on the overnight train were taken so he ordered a "special" train just for him so he could have an "upper" berth. He did not get the yacht.

The yacht **KILKENNY**, after Crozier's ownership, became the official yacht of the United State Commerce Department. It was made available to the Secretary of Commerce for his official and personal use. In 1920, the **KILKENNY** went through the Chesapeake and Delaware Canal. While passing under the "Buck Bridge", the topmast head was sheared off and all the rigging fell to the deck. The masts of modern style sailing ships were not single spars, but were constructed of separate sections or masts, bound together and each with its own rigging. This accident would have required a great deal of repair.

By 1932, President Hoover had the **SEQUOIA** for the Presidential yacht and the Commerce Department had the **KILKENNY**. Hoover was on an extended working vacation in Florida that included a flotilla of other boats including the **KILKENNY**. Unfortunately, the shallow waters of Florida made for difficult travel as the **SEQUOIA** and the **KILKENNY** each touched bottom on occasion. The Presidential fishing trip was significantly impacted as the President could not reach the sailfish fishing grounds.

As the Depression raged on, Hoover sold the Presidential yacht, the Secretary of the Navy's yacht and sent the **KILKENNY** to Florida for service under the bureau of steamship inspection. When Roosevelt became President, he ordered that an updated **SEQUOIA** was to be commandeered for use by the President. However, before the **SEQUOIA** could be put back into official use, Roosevelt took the Commerce Department's **KILKENNY** for his temporary use.

The fate of the **KILKENNY** is unknown. It was probably pressed into wartime use and then sold by the US government after the war, but that is only speculation given that most large yachts were taken by the government for the war effort.

REOLA built in 1912; owned by Olds from 1912 to 1915

By 1910, R.E. Olds had decided on upon a nautical lifestyle that would continue for the next 30 plus years. He would own two yachts, usually one "up north" in Michigan and one in Florida. Some years he owned 3 or even 4 yachts.

Source: Olds Family Archives – Ed Roe

The **REOLA** was designed by Cox & Stevens in 1910 and built the next year by the New York Yacht, Launch & Engine Company. A wooden yacht, she was launched for the 1912 yachting season. The **REOLA** was another shallow draft cruiser that Olds found exceptionally useful for Florida waters. Her length was 60 feet, the beam 13 feet 8 inches and the yacht's draft of approximately 3 feet allowed the captain to negotiate inland waterways and dock at shallow water ports. The captain was supported by a crew of 2 mates. **REOLA's** signal letters were LBQV.

The **REOLA** was equipped with a single 20th Century 4 cylinder 4 cycle gas engine that produced 50 horsepower.

The yacht design that Olds preferred was a combination of a houseboat and a motor cruiser. While perhaps an unusual design at that time in Florida, they were exceedingly comfortable in many regards. The **REOLA** had a raised deck which allowed for maximum cabin light and ventilation combined with a significant amount of deck space as the Olds' were frequently hosting guests and parties. The design utilized a trunk cabin style of construction which allowed for cabins to utilize the entire width of the yacht for maximum comfort. Similarly, the top of the cabin or main deck was also fully functional. The helm was open and thus afforded more open space to the Olds' and their guests.

By the end of 1915, the **REOLA** had been sold to W. Bartley Henry of Rosemont, Pa. The 1917 edition of Lloyd's Register of American Yachts listed the **REOLA** as being owned by Raymond L. Whitman of Boston, Mass.

> Historical fact: *Raymond L. Whitman was an interesting man in his own right. He was an inventor and partner in a telephone manufacturing business in 1895. By 1898, Whitman's telephone company was in the telephone exchange business and was the only incorporated phone company of its kind in Massachusetts. However, it was Whitman's inventions that are most interesting. The January 6th 1919 issue of the Palm Beach Post refers to one of Whitman's inventions: a coin sorter and wrapper. He offered it to the government for their use, and in logic that only can only be attributable to bureaucratic thinking, the government turned the invention down because it "would deprive ex-soldiers and other government clerks of occupations and livelihood". Whitman's other notable invention was a golf hole renovator, an apparatus that trimmed the golf hole thus making for clean edges.*

Early in 1917, **REOLA** had changed ownership again. This time she was owned by W. F. Favorite of Atlantic City and Palm Beach. The Palm Beach Post of January 29, 1917 noted the arrival of the "handsome **REOLA** which lies at the east end of the high bridge is a remarkably handsome boat – and there are few vessels reaching these waters more perfectly fitted". The **REOLA** made the Post again the following week because one of the female passengers lost a platinum and diamond ring near the yacht. A reward was offered for its return.

> Historical fact: *W.F. Favorite employed Captain Starn as the ship's captain. Captain Starn was well known in Atlantic City for his cruise ships and restaurant. As a young man, Starn was a lifeguard in Atlantic City and had saved one W.F. Favorite. Favorite had a boat built for Starn but insisted the boat be named the W.F. Favorite! That boat gave Starn the means to start fishing charters. The business grew through the years to include a fleet of deep sea fishing boats, daily excursion vessels, a fishing pier with a seafood restaurant and market, speedboat rides on the "MISS ATLANTIC CITY" and occasional tourist exhibits of marine life.*

In 1950, The **REOLA**, now called the **VAHALLA II**, was written up in a Fort Myers, FL newspaper in a human interest story. At this point, the owner was Captain Sid Smith. In a column called **Along the Waterfront**, Captain Hall wrote about the yacht and some of the unique features he saw:

"The designer had some unorthodox ideas, which worked out well indeed...On most boats of this size, the engineer has to take the engine room apart to get into it. Then the rest of the crew have to take the engineer apart to get him out. But the engine room in the VAHALLA II has full headroom with a great variety of electrically driven tools – emery wheels, buffers, drills, etc. ranging along the bulkheads, a complete little machine shop. From the high wheelhouse, the pilot has perfect vision in all directions, pilothouse controls and engine room telegraph, radio and ship-to-shore telephone."

Olds was showing that he indeed knew how to plan his yachts for maximum space and utilization. He would continue to have more and more input into each of his succeeding yachts.

The current whereabouts of the **VAHALLA II/ REOLA** is unknown.

By 1910, at the age of 46, Olds had started the process of pulling back from the automobile business. He was far wealthier than he ever imagined and started looking for other ways to ensure his legacy. In the ensuing years, he started the first private foundation in Michigan (1914), now called the R.E. Olds Foundation and still run by his heirs. By 1915, Olds gave up his title of General Manager and retained the Presidency of the REO Companies until 1923 when he became Chairman. Olds was quite pleased with this transition as it suited his desires to pursue his interests in other areas.

Olds was becoming quite interested in real estate. Initially he purchased land and buildings in the Central Michigan area. He also looked for ways to showcase his wealth to his fellow industrialists. Ever the practical man, his real estate purchases often had a business side to them. For example, his purchase in 1917 of a large portion of Grosse Ile on the Detroit River was not only for building a lavish Italianate mansion called Elbamar (it is still in existence and privately owned), Elbamar also became a working farm for testing his new inventions, such as the power lawn mower. Many of his farming ideas were tested at Elbamar by the farm manager and then transferred to Oldsmar in Florida, his major real estate project. Elbamar was a working farm as well as a place to entertain his business colleagues. While Elbamar was "just" a summer & fall home, it played an important role in the agricultural business model planned for Oldsmar, one of Olds' greatest endeavors. The following photograph shows a launch at Elbamar.

Source: Olds Family Archives – Ed Roe

Oldsmar: acquired in 1916 and sold starting in 1923

Entitled: Frolicing (sic) in the surf at Oldsmar (ca early 1920's)
source: Flickr; (no know copyright)

One of the typical efforts to market the lifestyle and beauty of Oldsmar, Florida.

Oldsmar was R.E. Olds' grand experiment in urban planning. Olds long had planned to invest in Florida real estate, first for his residence and then as a speculative investment. He had hoped to build a unique city comprised of agricultural, industrial and residential bases. His plans included a hotel, docks, beach and to draw upon other natural aspects of Florida. In fact, Olds also hoped to create a lifestyle and living environment for the working (middle) class that had never been contemplated before. In fact, he advertised Oldsmar with the slogan: "Oldsmar for Health, Wealth and Happiness".

The **REOLA II** (see page 36) was built to be his Florida yacht as a base for his operations while in Florida. The yacht was suited for his social and business needs.

Olds correctly forecast the Florida real estate boom. However he incorrectly timed his entry and the scope of his development given the recent world war and the US economic situation. His plan became totally unrealistic in reality and cost him dearly. But he was also early in exiting Florida real estate after he realized that his goals would not be met. The Florida real estate bubble wouldn't burst for another few years in 1926. Olds still lost a significant amount of money but it could have been much, much worse.

Yet, had the timing and world conditions been different, Oldsmar might have become the template for many other cities. In reality, Olds' dream was not realistic given the timing (post-world war and recession). To move to Oldsmar either as an employer or employee was risky and unlike moving today to a new location to start a new career. Those wishing to farm plots at Oldsmar faced especially unique risks associated with farming.

Olds lost, after liquidating the Oldsmar assets, nearly $3,000,000 of his personal fortune. Using the US Government's CPI Inflation calculator, this was the equivalent of nearly $48 million dollars in 2018. By 1923, Olds had nearly divested himself of the Oldsmar investment. The crash in Florida real estate which would set Florida back for decades wouldn't occur for another 3 years. In fact, Florida's economy did not recover until after World War II. Please read Chapter 5 for a more detailed discussion of Oldsmar.

REOMAR II: built in 1912; owned by Olds from 1912 to 1922

By 1910, R.E. Olds and his REO Motor Car Company were again leaders in the industry. While Olds Motor Works foundered under the leadership of the Smiths and was subsequently sold to Durant to create General Motors, Olds was having the time of his life. His marketing prowess (Baby REO, transcontinental trips, President Roosevelt's ride in a REO) once again helped separate his company from the nearly 1,200 other automobile manufacturers in the country. The REO's performance in the Glidden Reliability Tour proved that his car was a roadworthy and dependable vehicle. Dependability of the REO became such a concern to Olds, perhaps because of the memories of the problems with the early Curved Dash Olds, that production was often held down much to the dismay of the sales force. Olds could have easily followed other higher volume auto manufacturers and gone for volume over quality. Olds seemed less concerned about his sales ranking as time went on. As his market share slipped away to Ford and GM, he seemed unfazed as he turned his vision and energy towards other goals.

During this time, he continued to start numerous other companies, many of them to feed the growing REO enterprise. (see footnote at the end of this chapter) He also started during this period to branch out in his investments and interests. He founded Capital National Bank in Lansing, MI (1906). He joined the Board of Kalamazoo College and remained on the board until his death in 1950.

However, unlike how success and prosperity were associated with Olds, the *REOMAR II* had a completely different story. This vessel was visited by disaster in its initial start and again at the end of its run. Construction of the *REOMAR II* started in 1910 and was ready to launch in the spring of 1911. However the ship (and the boat factory) caught fire before completion and the yacht burned to the waterline. Olds then commissioned the builder to start again. Like the earlier yachts, the *REOMAR II* was designed by Cox & Stevens and built by the New York Yacht, Launch & Engine Co. of New York.

Source: Power Boating, 1914

Source: Olds Family Archives - Stephens

After the initial hull for the **REOMAR II** burned in 1911, the Olds family went on a vacation to Alaska instead. Meanwhile, Olds ordered the yacht to be built according to the same specifications. The official Lloyd's Register of American Yachts designation for the **REOMAR II** was a "Screw Steamer Schooner". The yacht continued the trunk cabin theme without the raised deck. The helm and main salon were enclosed which were required since this yacht was going to be doing service in the northern states.

REOMAR II, a wooden hull, was 98 feet LOA with a beam or width of 15 feet 6 inches. Her depth was 4 feet, a more moderate draft that would allow her to "go north". She was powered by two Winton engines (made by his old friend and fellow auto manufacturer, Alexander

Winton) each being a 6 cylinder, 4 stroke. The engines were designed to put out 100 horsepower. The yacht weighted 79 tons gross. She operated with a crew of 9.

Below is a photograph of the **REOMAR II**'s crew; the exact date is unknown. Based upon the clothing, there were at least 4, maybe 5, officers and 4 crew mates.

Source: Olds Family Archives - Stephens

Accommodations were spacious and ample room was provided for owner and guest alike. The usual layout was two large staterooms for Mr. & Mrs. Olds, two large staterooms aft for the guests with two large bathrooms for the onboard party.

In 1912, the newly constructed **REOMAR II** was picked up by the captain and crew at the builder's shipyard in Morris Heights, New York City. They then proceeded to Old Point Comfort in Hampton, VA. The Olds family and guests left Lansing, Michigan on a special rail car and met the new yacht and crew there. The cruising party went up the East Coast to Boston where it picked up Gladys Olds, the oldest daughter of R.E. and Metta Olds, who was attending The Dana Hall School. The yacht then proceeded to the St. Lawrence River on its way to the Great Lakes. The family used the **REOMAR II** extensively during the summer of 1912. A newspaper article in September, 1912 reported the return of the **REOMAR II** as she returned from a 6 months cruise starting in the Chesapeake Bay and tributaries to Martha's Vineyard. The yacht then proceeded to Nova Scotia, then up the St. Lawrence River, Thousand Islands and Lake Erie before arriving at Detroit. She was moored for the winter in Port Clinton, Ohio.

Source: Olds Family Archives - Stephens

During 1912, REO advertised the famous R.E. Olds "Farewell" ad. The ad, which refers to Olds as a "designer" claiming that "I do not believe a car materially better will ever be built" and "this car marks my limit" and "So I've called it My Farewell Car". Olds himself was concerned that that auto buyers might think he was leaving the company. The copy writer convinced Olds that people would focus on the quality of the car based upon Olds' reputation and not draw the wrong conclusion. This ad campaign was in fact critical to the company's success. Automobile production had fallen by over 20% and the dividend was omitted for the first time in the company's history. It should be noted that Olds as the majority owner of REO Motor Car Co. enjoyed the benefits of the significant dividends the company paid. The "Farewell" ad appeared in publications with a combined circulation of 30,000,000 readers; it was the largest advertising drive in the history of the automobile industry to date. It worked, automobile sales rose 22% the following year.

Interestingly, Henry Ford, R.E. Olds and the other early automotive pioneers had uniquely different approaches to running their businesses. It has been written that very few early investors in the auto industry made money. Ford and Olds were the clear exceptions. Ford wanted to remove his investors as soon as possible and then redeploy the profits of the business into growing the business. R. E. Olds, perhaps because of the concern about being poor or of losing his business again, paid out substantial dividends in stock and cash. Olds' personal files contain letters, especially a poignant one from a Civil War widow, which praised his generosity and goodness. Of course this generosity also benefited him as he built a substantial personal net worth outside the REO business but this also was a considerable drain on the resources of the REO Motor Car Company and its ability to stay competitive.

> *Historical fact*: The Dodge brothers owned 10% of the Ford Motor Company in 1916. Ford had a capital surplus of $60 million, worth $1.4 billion in 2017. Ford decided to end any dividends and redeploy them into the business investments, hiring and salaries. Ford believed this was in the best interests of the business. However, the Dodge brothers objected stating that Ford should stop reducing prices on his cars since they couldn't meet the current orders and continue to pay the dividends. Ford long suspected the Dodge brothers were using "his" dividends to create their own car company (Ford was right). The lawsuit was about whether minority shareholders could prevent management from operating the company for profitable <u>and charitable</u> purposes. The Dodge brothers won the case and forced an extra dividend of $19.3 million to all shareholders. As a result of this decision, Ford threatened to start a new competing company as a way to force the Dodge brothers to sell. It worked, the Dodge brothers sold their shares but the proceeds were used to establish and grow the Dodge Brothers Company. Since that time, courts have ruled the management and boards have very expansive powers to make any rational decision that will, in their opinion, benefit the corporation.

In 1913, the family wintered in the West Indies aboard the yacht. The **REOMAR II** was then brought to Northern Michigan where the family spent the summer cruising the bays and harbors with friends. In fact, one friend of the Olds family sent a letter to a local paper describing the generosity of the Olds' and the fun the large group was having. In one incident, the **REOMAR II** was moored off Roaring Brook, near Harbor Springs, MI. As the writer put it: *"the natives of the beach were having a hilarious time in swimming. The welcome according to the Reomar was so vociferous that the Reomartians were for a time in doubt as to what tribe of Indians they had discovered."*

The **REOMAR II** spent its remaining time with the Olds family traveling the Great Lakes and the East Coast of the US. In 1922, the Olds family, while in Southport, Connecticut, visited Gutzon Borglum, the carver of the Presidents' heads at Mt. Rushmore. The yacht was traded shortly thereafter for the Kenmoor Apartment building in Detroit. There may have been other considerations given to R.E. beyond the apartment building but the details of that transaction have been lost to history.

The Kenmoor Apartments was a building located in Detroit, Michigan. There were 34 apartments in a building newly constructed in 1922. The building was 53'3" X 124' X 40'. It was a three story brick building with a full basement. The building was eventually torn down and the lots are still vacant as of today.

Interestingly, in 1923, Olds had no yachts that year; undoubtedly the result of the challenging times that he was going through personally but probably more than likely due to timing delays in his newest yacht, the 98 foot, **REOMAR III.**

Two years after Olds traded the yacht, the final disaster struck the **REOMAR II**. While in port in Toledo, Ohio, the **REOMAR II** (second hull) also caught fire on June 28, 1924 with 4 crewmembers aboard. Fortunately, the crew survived but the yacht was a total loss.

Source: Hamilton, Ohio Journal News June 27, 1924

However, there was much more to the story of "why" the **REOMAR II** burned. After Olds' ownership, one D. C. Stephenson of Indiana purchased the yacht for a reputed $55,000 (nearly $780,000 in 2018), a huge sum for a yacht. Stephenson is now a footnote in history but in 1922, he was the Grand Dragon of the Ku Klux Klan in Indiana. He eventually became one of the most powerful Klan leaders in the country. He was controlling and abusive with his power and often attacked those that challenged him. He was flamboyant and loved to show off his wealth; the **REOMAR II** was his stage.

In the early morning hours of June 27, 1924, the **REOMAR II** lay quietly at anchor at the Toledo Yacht Club. Two horrific explosions occurred. Three crew members narrowly avoided being caught below deck and another crew member was blown from the deck but caught a side rail. After the first explosion, the crew members got into a row boat and got safely away from the yacht before the second explosion occurred. While guards and crews from other boats attempted to fight the fire, the stiff winds assisted the fire in growing and consuming the yacht. According to the local newspaper account, "only a blackened spar remained of one of the finest yachts on the Great Lakes".

As it turned out, Stephenson was a targeted man. This was an assassination attempt, however Stephenson was not on the yacht. He wielded power and assisted those that supported him and crushed those in his way. As a result, he made many enemies. Stephenson became anxious and paranoid about assassination. He hired & fired many bodyguards and tried to avoid becoming a target in public. His conduct became more unstable as a result of excessive drinking. He sued the Ku Klux Klan Imperial Wizard and the Grand Dragon of the Indiana realm for conspiring to destroy his yacht in October, 1924. He sued the Klan leaders for $125,000 in damages. By this time, Stephenson had left the Klan after quarrelling with the leaders of the group.

John H. Brady of Muncie, Indiana, a former cleaner and dyer by trade, was arrested on December 15, 1924 for setting fire to *REOMAR II*. Brady was a small time criminal with a long record for liquor law violations and automobile theft. According to the newspaper account, Brady admitted that he alone was responsible for the fire. However, on December 17th, Brady's "confession" fell apart when police found out he was 400 miles away from Toledo on the day of the fire. Brady then stated he had been picked to be the "goat". He said he agreed to shoulder the blame and "he would be taken care of". Brady was released and never charged for the yacht burning. He returned home to Muncie, Indiana and was arrested for a series of home burglaries the following year.

Stephenson's lawsuit against the former Klan leaders was dismissed in May, 1925 when Stephenson's attorney failed to show for a scheduled hearing. No one was ever arrested for the crime of setting the *REOMAR II* on fire.

Stephenson was arrested a year later for the rape and murder of a young woman. He was sentenced to life in prison.

REOLA II: built in 1914; owned by Olds from 1915 to 1923

In 1914, Olds commissioned another yacht with Cox & Stevens. She was to be called the **REOLA II** and would replace the **REOLA**. This yacht was an 80 foot shallow water cruiser to be used primarily in Florida. Olds had become very pleased with this type of trunk cabin cruiser, with a raised deck, combining the best attributes of a houseboat and motor yacht per Yachting Magazine of December, 1914. Lloyd's Register of American Yachts in 1917 listed the **REOLA II** as a Screw Steamer Schooner.

Source: Olds Family Archives - Stephens

This yacht was also built by the New York Yacht, Launch & Engine Company. Constructed with a wooden hull, she was 80 feet LOA with a beam of 16 feet and a draft of 3 feet 2 inches. Olds had learned that a shallower draft boat allowed him more access to locations in the Florida waters, especially given the tides. As such, the hull was almost flat bottomed amidships. The power was two 50 horsepower Sterling gas motors, each engine being 4 stroke, 4 cylinder. She was designed for a crew of eight. **REOLA II's** signal letters were LFKM.

The design of the first **REOLA** was created to accommodate the need for windows offering light and, especially, ventilation for the staterooms in the southern states. **REOLA II** offered a maximum of canvas covered deck space for guests. However, Olds undoubtedly found that the quick pop-up storms of the south required the ability to seek shelter on board.

The architect designed the vessel so as much of the beam of the boat could be used by Olds and his guests. The entire trunk cabin was usable as well as the deck to the stern. Even the walk way around the trunk cabin was narrowed so as to provide more space to the passengers. The **REOLA II** stern was wider than normal to provide additional room and accommodations. The forward deckhouse contained a large dining room. Just aft of the deckhouse was the galley; the top of the galley was used as a navigating bridge for the yacht. Below the upper deck was a large salon; the rooms for the Olds' and their guests surrounded the salon. The Olds staterooms were forward of the salon and were wide with built-in berths, two large wardrobes, a bureau, dressing table and a settee. The use of multiple windows allowed for comfortable ventilation and lighting. The salon had a piano, music rack and writing table on the port side. The starboard side had a large lounge upholstered in leather. The accommodations for the passengers were smaller but just as comfortably designed as the Olds' staterooms.

The design included excellent ventilation for the engines thus not affecting any passengers.

REOLA II docked at the Olds family home in Daytona Beach, FL
Source: Olds Family Archives - Stephens

Source: Olds Family Archives – Ed Roe

A very rare shot of the **REOLA II** and the **REOMAR II** docked together

A typical lunch on board the **REOLA II**. The Olds' loved to have large groups cruise with them. R.E. Olds is hidden in the photo. Note the dingy to the right with the yacht's name.

Source: Olds Family Archives - Stephens

Each of Olds' yachts contained improvements that Olds had learned from his prior yachts and his yachting experiences. Olds was a uniquely creative man and he was actively involved in the designing of all his yachts.

REOLA II was launched in July 6, 1915 at the Morris Heights shipyard of The New York Yacht, Launch & Engine Co. The entire Olds family boarded the yacht in New York, cruised to Philadelphia, then on to the Chesapeake and up the Potomac to Washington.

According to the ship's log, the heat and humidity was terrific during the trip so the ship's design provided some comfort to the travelers.

The yacht was launched uneventfully on July 6, 1915 at 5 PM. The next two weeks were a scene of slightly organized mass chaos as plumbers, carpenters, machinists, electricians, pipe fitters, painters and upholsterers all jockeyed for space to finish their work so the family could leave on their trip on July 20th. The entry in the ships log for Friday July 9 summed up the situation:

9 – Friday. Found leak in saloon companion way owning to weight of mast. Must keep stanchion in place. Pipe fitter finished up galley, upholsterer putting down carpets, put cushions and mattresses on board. Terrible confusion – painter painting floor – electrician at work. Tested out deck engines all night. Wish I could stay aboard. (source: REOLA II Ships log; entry by ship's master). The ships log make for fascinating reading of life, from the perspective of captain, on a yacht.

On Saturday the 17th, **REOLA II** was taken out for a test run. The clutch for the port engine failed and the ship eventually limped back to the shipyard awaiting parts. On the 19th, the parts arrived and one crew member quit. A replacement was found that day. On the morning of the 20th with the Olds family on board, the new steward joined the yacht. The yacht cast off at 10 AM only to have the engines stall. However, this problem was short lived and soon the family was on their way to Sayreville, NJ for the first stop. The ship's master dryly noted in the log "Not quite as smooth engine as I would like".

The larger yacht was more conducive to Olds' life style as he was spending more and more time in Florida managing his Oldsmar investment. In fact, most of 1917 was spent in Florida dealing with a growing number of issues surrounding the Oldsmar development, located near Tampa and still in existence. The **REOLA II** was well suited for social events as well as family cruises.

The **REOLA II** had a very unusual feature for its time. Aft of the main saloon/salon were two unusually large rooms with bathrooms attached at their aft end. Forward of the saloon/salon was the same arrangement. The central saloon/salon contained a large and easily accessed staircase to the upper deck. The forward staterooms belonged to the Olds'. The saloon/salon contained a piano, music rack, writing desk, large lounge chairs and a locker for fishing rods and guns.

The ship's log gives a tremendous insight into the living conditions and life for the crew aboard the yacht. The yacht was typically used by the family for 2 to 3 months a year. Other friends from Lansing, Michigan, relatives and Florida friends all used the yacht at the invitation of Olds. However, there were months where the crew was stationed on the yacht with nothing to do but maintain the ship. Because of the demand on Olds' time, he often forgot to pay the crew. There are several entries where the ship's master ran out of money and the crew was forced to go without or established credit locally in order to eat and have provisions. All crew were paid eventually but one senses the frustration coming from the ship's master after sending repeated telegrams requesting money.

Thanksgiving Day, 1915. Have plenty to be thankful for, but wish we could get underway again – as it is tiresome doing nothing.

January 19, 1916. Wednesday. Mr. Olds arrived about 6pm after an absence of 5 months and 6 days. Long time doing nothing.
(source: REOLA II ship's log; entry by ship's master)

From the entries in the ship's log, it is clear that when the Olds' were on board, life was much different. Olds always had a large group of guests on board and treated guests and crew alike extremely well. In fact, 3 days after the January 19th entry, the **REOLA II** departed for a day trip to Turtle Mound, FL with 29 people on board, including 27 guests of the Olds'.

When the Olds' were not on board, things still got quite interesting. On March 4, 1916, Mr. & Mrs. Wallace Olds (brother of R.E) and Mrs. Sarah Sheets (sister of R.E) departed the **REOLA II** after cruising for several weeks. A new party of 5 (unnamed in the ship's log) came aboard for a week's cruise. Two trunks of the guests fell into the water and the crew and captain had a very difficult time retrieving them. Needless to say, the contents were quite wet and to the amusement of the ship's captain, the "ship was decorated all day with clothing drying".

The last entry in the ship's log was for April 11, 1916. The ship was being put up for the summer and the ship's master was going home. He noted that he had drilled two holes in the garboard (the immediate planks on either side of the keel) to allow the draining of the dirty oil out of the bilge. His last notation was: *"Do not forget that two (2) holes drilled in the engine room to let dirt drain out. Watch before putting overboard."*

Here is an ad from April 1923 by which Olds' would have procured the help for the yacht.

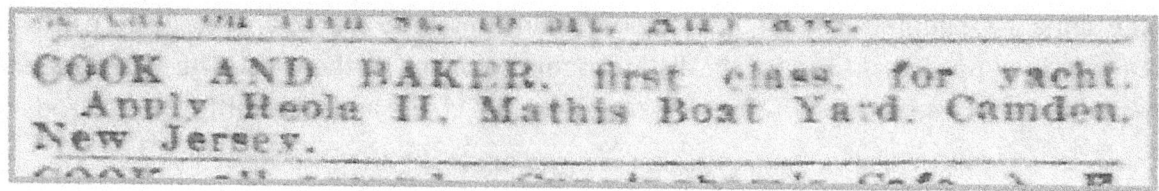

Source: Philadelphia Inquirer, April 19, 1923

The ***REOLA II*** remained in the Olds family until mid-1923 when it was sold. There is some family lore that the yacht was traded, but Olds' notes indicate that he sold it to J.R. Wotherspoon of Philadelphia. Mr. Wotherspoon was a stove manufacturer and salesman. He renamed the yacht ***FEDORA.***

In December of 1923, an article about arriving yachts in Palm Beach includes a description of the ***FEDORA***, formerly the ***REOLA II***. The article mentions the yacht will proceed to Miami, which will be her winter headquarters for cruises.

Interestingly, the next mention of the ***FEDORA***, now called the ***EDORA*** is in the Chicago Tribune of January 9, 1928 listing the assets of The Sanitary District of Chicago. It is not clear why she was acquired by the Sanitary District or what her purpose was for them. Was she a working ship or a pleasure craft for management? Also, the name change from ***FEDORA*** to ***EDORA*** is peculiar. The connection between the ***REOLA II*** and the ***EDORA*** was verified from the U. S. Merchant Vessel List of 1927.

Also listed are her annual operating expenses:

Captain, 1 at $3,000.00
Engineer, 1 at $2,700.00
Deck Hands, 2 at $2,200 each
Watchmen, 2 at $2,200 each.

Annual operating expenses were $14,580.00 or $212,000 in 2018.

The ***EDORA*** is listed as 90 horsepower down from the original power plants totaling 100 horsepower. Also the ***EDORA*** was refitted for her new service with the Sanitary District. She was 12 feet longer, now with a length overall of 95 feet and her beam was 19 feet versus the original 16 feet. She was now housed a crew of eight.

No record remains of the whereabouts of the ***REOLA II/FEDORA/ EDORA***.

After the sale of the ***REOLA II***, Olds only maintained one yacht, the ***REOMAR II***, on the Great Lakes until 1922. However, Olds was about to build even larger yachts as he continued to drift away from the REO Motor Car Co. operations.

R.E. Olds was now entering the 1920's, a period of unprecedented economic growth. Olds was 56 and had just sold The Michigan Screw Company in 1919 for $1mm; his original investment was $10,000. Olds had long since started his transition away from the auto industry. He was much more interested in his other investments and endeavors, such as yachting.

The following is a partial list of his business investments:

-National Coil Co. (1904, became part of REO in 1918)
-Michigan Screw Co. (1906 – 1934); owed by Olds until 1919
-Air Cooled Motor Co.
-The Original Gas Engine Co. – Later Ideal Power Lawn Mower Co. (Olds invented the power lawn mower)
-Kold-Hold Mfg Co.
-Capital National Bank
-Olds Tower
-Olds Hotel
-Atlas Drop Forge Co.
-Hill Diesel Engine Co.
-REO Motor Truck Company

"Only those who risk going too far can possibly find out how far they can go"
T.S. Eliot

CHAPTER THREE

TRANSITION YEARS
1921 TO 1940

If a man is to be obsessed by something, I suppose a boat is as good as anything, perhaps a bit better than most.

E.B. White

In the early 1920's, sales volume at The REO Company for cars and trucks had decreased significantly which certainly was another distraction weighing heavily upon Olds. Olds was heavily dependent upon REO dividends to support his life style and build his net worth. Now this source of income was in question. Olds had always wisely built and invested his cash reserves. It has been said by many that he had a fear of being poor again, a totally understandable emotion for one who came up from such a poor background.

1923 was a year of transition for Olds when he realized that his lofty goals for Oldsmar were not going to be met, certainly not any time that fit within his financial parameters. By 1923, Olds had also sold the **REOMAR II** and the **REOLA II**.

By 1923, Olds had invested nearly $4 million of his fortune into Oldsmar. That amount equates to nearly $58.3 million in 2018 before liquidation. Oldsmar was proving to be more than Olds could handle and he began to sell and trade his investment in Oldsmar to stop his losses. Olds' net loss was $3.0 million. Today, Oldsmar is a thriving community reflecting the vision and values that R.E. Olds envisioned for it. It would be a city he would be proud of today.

Without Oldsmar, Olds' land development plans were ended. Elbamar, his summer home in Michigan outside Detroit on Grosse Ile, was no longer needed as a proving ground for his farm operations in Oldsmar nor did he need Elbamar for his business socializing as he was also reducing his involvement in the REO Company business. 1923 also saw Olds give up the Presidency of REO Motor Co for the honorary title of Chairman of the Board. Personally, Olds was comfortable with the change of direction in his life. As he did many other times, he could simply change direction and take his life in a different direction: selling Elbamar and looking for a more private retreat in Northern Michigan was soon to be part of that change. Yachting was always to be part of his plans from now on until his death.

Elbamar was eventually offered to Henry Ford and other wealthy Detroit industrialists. The island had become a retreat for Detroit's wealthy but it was not an easy sell.

Source: Olds Family Archives – Stephens

It was offered for sale as a men's sporting club and eventually to the public as the real estate was broken into parcels and sold off. The Olds' main house was used as a USO center during World War II. Today it is privately owned and has been converted into an apartment building. It has been lovingly maintained and retains much of its charm.

REOMAR III: launched in 1924, owned from 1924 to 1931

After the tumultuous early years of the early 1920's, Olds was exhausted and wanted to travel again. He had been involved in numerous activities, both business and personal over the previous decade. He took his family on an extended 6 month trip around the world. However, he was not to be far from another yacht. As was his practice, he had decided in 1922 to build another yacht.

1924 brought the arrival of the **REOMAR III**. Designed by Cox & Stevens and built by the Defoe Boat & Motor Works of Bay City, Michigan, she was the first steel hulled yacht for Olds. Defoe had contacted Olds when hearing that Olds was considering a new yacht. Defoe Boat & Motor Works started in 1905 as a partnership between brothers H.J. & F.W. Defoe and a brother-in-law. The initial contract price for the **REOMAR III** was $25,000, however Olds was always modifying his plans as he devised further refinements and improvements so rarely was the contract price the final price. Olds often was involved in many of the major and minor decision about the yachts: from the quality of the raw materials, including the choice of steel quality, to decorating decisions. Olds preferred the darker look of teak and especially mahogany for the trunk cabin. He also preferred a highly varnished finish. The crew typically spent their downtime, which could be 3 to 5 months at a stretch, varnishing the bright work on the yacht.

While many of his yachts, including the **REOMAR III**, were capable of ocean travel since they had a cruising range of 2,500 nautical miles, Olds stated he preferred coastal travel and inland water navigation where he claimed "I can get the most enjoyment out of life."

Source: Olds Family – Ed Roe

The **REOMAR III** at dock in Charlevoix, Michigan. Note the Olds boathouse behind the yacht.

Source: Olds Family – Ed Roe

Defoe Shipbuilding Company was considered to be an excellent small to medium size (around 100 ft.) ship builder. It did build torpedo chasers and mine planters for the US Navy in World War I. For World War II, it built destroyer escorts, patrol and landing craft. After the war ended, the company built several Great Lakes freighters as well as several ships for defense purposes. Defoe also built research vessels, most notably the **RV KNORR** which eventually found the wreck of the **RMS TITANIC**.

> Historical fact: *Most notably, in 1931, Defoe built the **LENORE**, a 92' yacht for Sewell Avery, chairman of Montgomery Ward department stores. It featured twin, 500-horsepower Winton (of automotive fame) diesel engines capable of churning the twin screws and generating speeds of 25 miles per hour. It was the fastest ship of its kind on the Great Lakes. The LENORE underwent several changes of names and eventually became the Presidential yacht for the President of the United States. Avery named it after his second daughter who died at the age of four; this yacht was taken by the U.S. Government in World War II for coastal picket duty by the Coast Guard, and in 1956 it was assigned as a Presidential Yacht. It was called the **Barbara Anne** by President Eisenhower after his granddaughter, the **Honey Fitz** by President Kennedy in honor of his maternal grandfather John Francis Fitzgerald, and the **Tricia** by President Nixon after his daughter.*

REOMAR III was built for 12 passengers and to be run by a crew of 6. Her dimensions were: LOA of 100' and LWL of 98'. The beam was 18'7" and the draft was 4'6". The depth was 8'. Interestingly, the Cox & Stevens, Inc. brochure for 1930 listed the crew requirement at 10. Olds was notorious among his crew for running his ships with less than the prescribed crew level. On most of his yachts, crewmen performed several functions.

The **REOMAR III** was fitted with a twin screw Mianus diesel engines with a total rated horsepower of 250 hp. Her cruising speed was 10 ½ knots and the cruising radius was 2,000 miles. The engine room also was equipped with an electric light generator (see Kohler ad comment below), ice machine, air compressor, fire pumps, water works motor, hot water system, and other items needed by the engineer. On the ceiling was two hydraulic cylinders which are controlled by a valve on the bridge to lift and lower the tenders (a 20 foot 4 cylinder runabout for the family and a 16 foot power tender for the crew). The yacht also had a small sail boat.

Source: Olds Family Archives – Stephens

Notably, the newspaper emphasized the amount of electric equipment the ship would carry. It also stated the yacht would be "equipped with a strong radio".

Just forward of the engine room is the mess room with the captain's quarters adjoining it. Forward of the mess room is the forecastle with the crew's sleeping quarters. The forecastle, also known as the fo'c's'le, is traditionally used for crew quarters and storage.

Historical fact: *Mianus Motor Works made diesel engines for the fishing industry in New England starting in the late 1890's. Diesel engines became popular for larger fishing fleets because of their fuel efficiency and simplicity. The diesel engines were being installed into sail powered offshore fishing vessels by the 1920s, first as an auxiliary engine to sails. Then, interestingly, sails became auxiliaries to engines. Trawling eventually became the main form of fishing because of the powerful engines and the ability to net large numbers of fish. Sailing vessels eventually disappeared.*

REOMAR III was christened Wednesday, November 21, 1923 in Bay City Michigan at the Defoe Shipbuilding Company shipyard. As reported in a Lansing, MI newspaper, the christening of the yacht was well attended. Peggy Anderson, the five year old granddaughter of Olds, formally christened the yacht. The yacht would be fitted out over the winter for a spring commissioning in June, 1924.

Courtesy: Lansing State Journal (November 27, 1923)

After the yacht was launched and christened, the **REOMAR III** cruised the Georgian Bay, the northern Great Lakes and the Thousand Islands that summer.

The yacht was designed for dual service: northern waters in the summer then Florida and the West Indies in the winter. A tourist brochure from the mid-1920's for Daytona, Florida shows the **REOMAR III** docked at the Daytona Yacht Club. The ship was constructed to have a large displacement, which in spite of a moderate draft, still rendered her as seaworthy. Interestingly, ports, not windows, were used for light and airflow. The ports were oversized to ensure adequate ventilation. The hull design was chosen to provide maximum topside deck space and large "roomy quarters" below deck. The owner's quarters were aft of the engine room while the officers and crew were forward of it.

The 50 foot teak deckhouse was created to provide for a large dining room and living room.

Source: Olds Family Archives - Stephens

Source: Olds Family Archives - Stephens

The dining room was 14 feet by 16 feet and finished in dark mahogany as Olds preferred. The Grosvenor Company of New York decorated the room with its large mahogany table, ten chairs and attractive wall decorations. Directly aft of the living room was the galley. The galley measured 7 feet by 14 feet and was well equipped with a refrigeration plant, electric dishwasher and "other modern conveniences" as stated in a local paper. Aft of the galley was the chart room and then a small passageway that allowed one to go to each side of the ship without going around the deckhouse.

The living room or lounge, by necessity, required a large amount of seating due to the number of guests on the yacht at any one time. The living room/lounge measured 14 feet by 22 feet. It was furnished with heavy soft chairs and sofas. In the corner of the lounge was a staircase leading to a lower corridor. The outside or after deck was 17 by 22 feet with a lower deck of 8 by 10 feet. All areas were large and roomy with ample accommodations for family and guests.

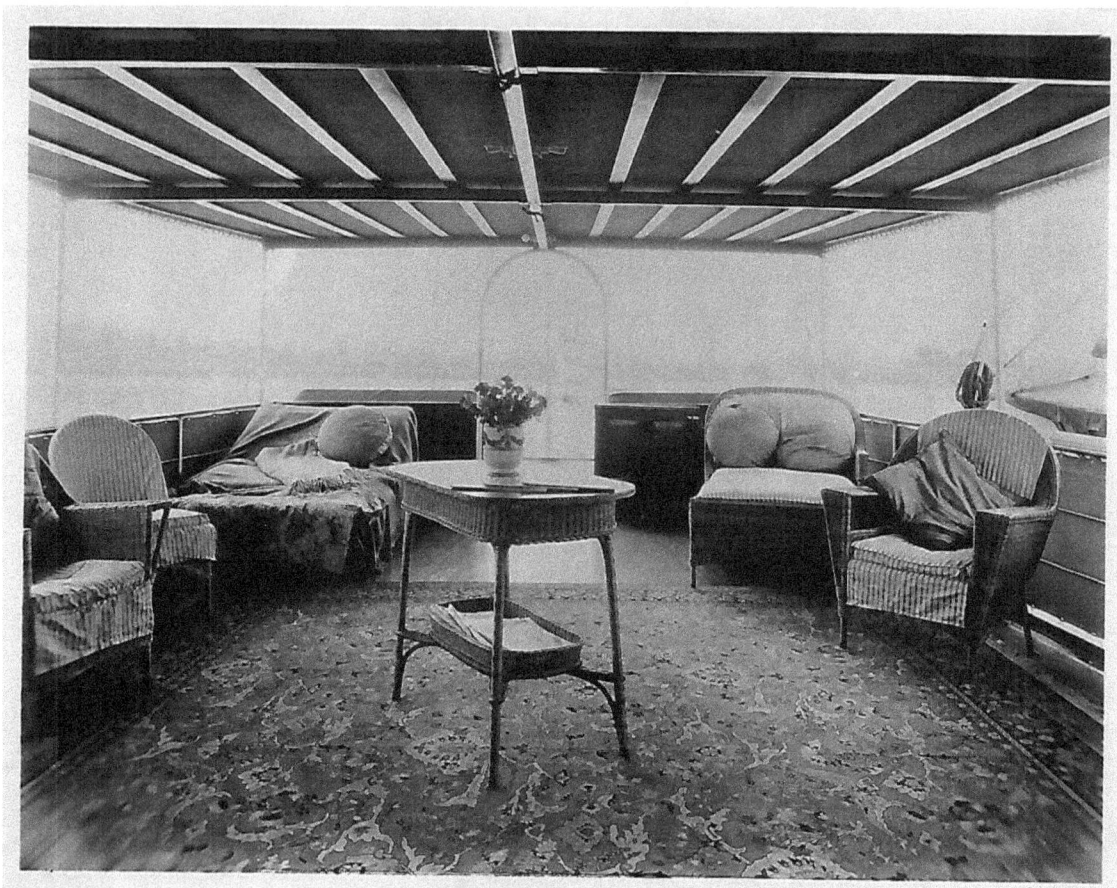

Source: Olds Family Archives – Stephens

The **REOMAR III** was outfitted with 6 staterooms and 5 baths. In the corner of the lounge was a stairway that led to a corridor below. Forward on the corridor was the Olds' stateroom which measured 11 feet by 18 feet. The same corridor was also the access to five double rooms. Four of the rooms were fitted with baths and the other two rooms are situated to so the occupants could use a toilet off the main corridor. The following is a photograph of a guest suite.

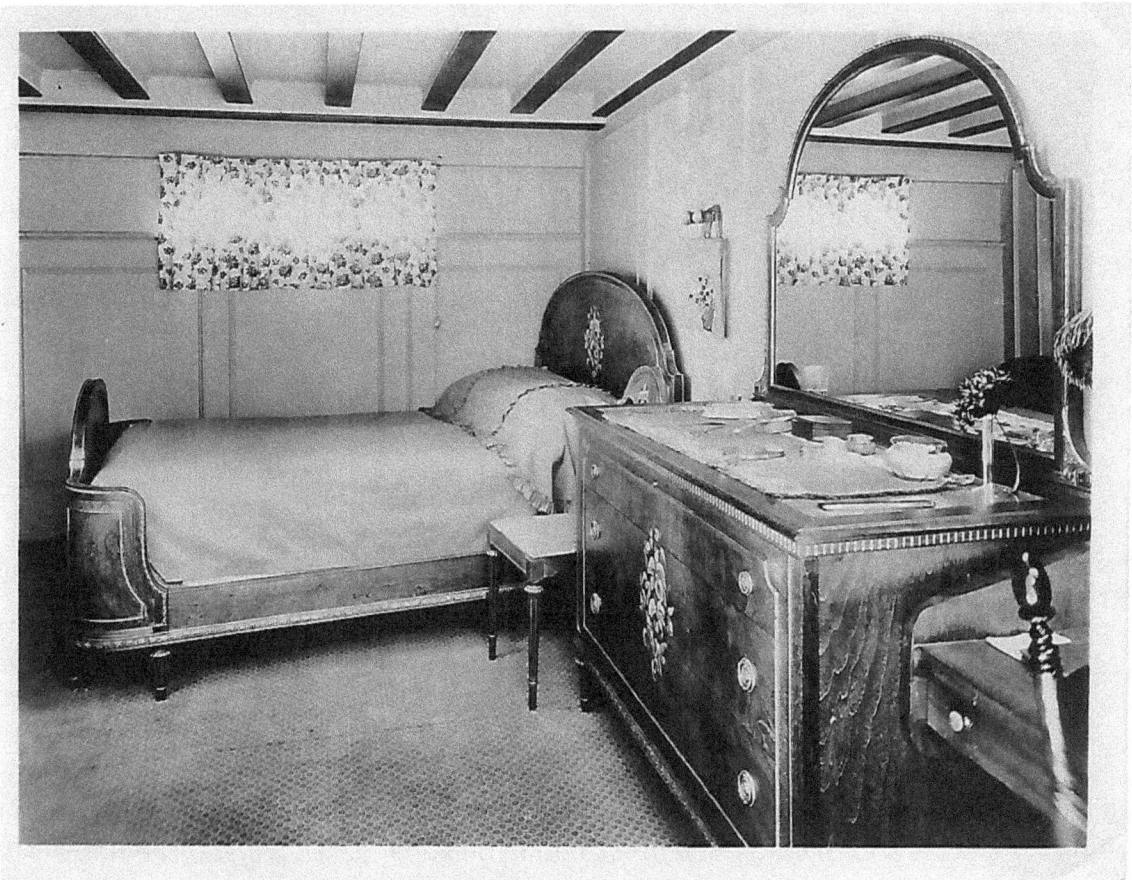

Source: Olds Family Archives – Stephens

Always the focal point on his yachts was a player piano. Olds, who was not an accomplished musician, nonetheless loved music and singing. He often led songfests and encouraged all to join in the fun. He always had a large hand cranked mahogany Victrola cabinet phonograph on his yachts for the same reason. The **REOMAR III** also had electric piano and a radio set. The lounge opened onto an after-deck which was 17 feet by 22 feet and a lower deck which was 8 feet by 10 feet. Olds always liked outside, covered seating area for his family and guests. This design provided a large area with plenty of seating. This outside area was well appointed with leather settees, a large Oriental rug and wicker furniture. There were usually two large daybeds for one or more people to recline for reading or relaxation. Olds preferred the darker colored woods and mahogany was usually his favorite choice even for the outside seating areas. He also liked the look of a heavily varnished finish. Olds was a stickler for details and often got involved in the detailed decorating decisions. From the type and finish of the interior hardware, table and bed linens to the china selection, he even designed the steel plate used to emboss the stationary for his yachts. One newspaper even wrote that Cox & Stevens, Olds' preferred yacht designer, created their designs from ideas suggested from Olds and his years of yachting and practical knowledge.

The following picture shows the Olds family and guests before leaving for a shore trip. Life on a yacht in the 1920's was much more formal than today.

Source: Olds Family Archives - Stephens

Yachting took a back seat to other endeavors for Olds during 1924 and 1925. The **REOMAR III** was his only yacht but Olds had focused his attention on yet another project: The Hotel Olds and the Capital National Bank, both in Lansing, Michigan.

The Hotel Olds was built in 1925 – 26 as part of a civic project by the appropriately named Lansing Community Hotel Corporation, largely funded by Olds. The hotel was designed by Holabird & Rood, noted architects of the day who also designed the Palmer House Hotel in Chicago. As previously noted, Olds typically immersed himself in the details of any project. In the Hotel Olds construction engineer's diary, now owned by the Olds descendants, are some very humorous stories about how they had to trick Mr. Olds into believing they were following his orders on quality & quantity of rebar and concrete for the hotel construction. Olds, who was in his mid-60's, was not above climbing up into the project site to inspect the workmanship.

Historical fact: *The Capital Bank Tower (now the Michigan National Tower) at 124-126 West Allegan Street was built in 1929-31 for R. E. Olds to house the R. E. Olds Company offices, the Capital National Bank, and rental office space. Significant as one of the last remaining structures in Lansing personally connected with R. E. Olds — probably the most important individual in Lansing's history — the tower is also notable as one of the finest 1920s office buildings in Michigan outside of Detroit.*

In 1927, an article appeared in a number of national newspapers stating that Olds had offered President Coolidge the use of their Charlevoix, MI cottage as well as the use of the *REOMAR III*. Olds later refuted that story saying the President had access to other properties and yachts.

Olds was now Chairman of REO Motors but spent most of his time focused upon personal investments like Hotel Olds, Bates & Edmonds Motor Company, Kalamazoo College (Chairman of the Board), traveling and yachting. Olds was in his 60's and clearly was enjoying the trappings of success that his great wealth brought him. By the end of the 1920's Olds would have more yachts (4) at one time than he had ever had before.

REOMAR III was used primarily in the North on the Great Lakes. *REOMAR III* saw limited duty in Florida, mostly she cruised the Great Lakes to the Thousand Islands in New York. Reportedly, *REOMAR III* in one cruising year, used over 2,000 gallons of diesel fuel during a cruising season of nearly 2,500 miles. The yacht was wintered in Charlevoix as was Olds' custom.

The *REOMAR III* even appeared in its own ad for Kohler Automatic Electric Plants. These small plants ran off a main generator and created 110-volt DC power. The unit was fully automatic so if a passenger wanted to turn on an electric light, it would start the electric plant immediately. R.E. Olds praised the electric plant in the ad on its quality of construction and lack of vibration.

Source: Olds Family Archives – Stephens

By 1926, Olds had purchased 150 acres in Northern Michigan near Charlevoix and started construction on a 17 bedroom log lodge, which he eventually named Oldswood. Ever mindful of yachting considerations, he selected Lake Charlevoix for its direct access to Lake Michigan. Here he could moor his favorite yacht protected from the potential storms and destruction from Lake Michigan. Oldswood was the summer location for a steady stream of visitors for the ultimate host: R.E. Olds.

> **Bonus historical fact**: *As Olds was prone to do, he loved being involved in multiple activities simultaneously. As his family would discover later when he felt he had truly retired, which was always a questionable issue with his family, he was a consummate host. He took to socializing as he did with his former business activities. The Olds yachts and homes were always full of people whenever they were "in residence". According to Gladys Olds Anderson and her son, R E Olds Anderson with verification from other family members, Olds maintained a constant flow of activities. Invitations were sent early in the year with a space for the addressee and another space for the week the Olds' wished them to visit and stay. The children and grandchildren also got to invite their friends (in limited numbers). Activities started early in the day and ran late: lawn bowling, swimming, cruising, water sports and singing around the piano. Select guests were invited on special occasions for costume parties. These were elaborate affairs and no expense was spared when one was invited to attend!*

Source: Olds Family Archives – Stephens

Olds soon had the opportunity to acquire the **SYLVIA IV**, another large yacht on Lake Charlevoix. Olds loved to trade and negotiate so soon the **REOMAR III** and cash were used to acquire the **SYLVIA IV**.

But the story of the **REOMAR III** was not yet over. In fact, the yacht survived until 2015 before it succumbed to the demolishing crew! Sadly the author and his wife were not able to locate the yacht in time before it was demolished.

The yacht **REOMAR III** was traded by Olds as part of the consideration for the purchase of the yacht **REOMAR IV**. **REOMAR III** was sold in 1931 to Alex J. Groesbeck, the former governor of

Michigan from 1921 – 1927. Groesbeck was known as an important advocate of road building in Michigan. He was the first governor in Michigan to champion the use of concrete and vowed to take Michigan out of the mud roads that were still far too prevalent in the early 1920's. Groesbeck only owned the **REOMAR III** for two years before selling to Charles Bidwell in late 1932.

Charles Bidwell was a colorful and extremely successful businessman and lawyer in Chicago. He was a well-known sports entrepreneur owning a racing stable, other sports related businesses and was President of the Chicago Stadium Operating Company. Purportedly, he had "ties" to organized crime and Al Capone (source: Wikipedia). See page 93 for further information on Al Capone and the stories of his purported ownership of two of Olds' yachts.

As we will see, two of Olds' yachts soon became loosely linked to Capone, perhaps as a result of those supposed ties of Bidwell. Further discussion of that association will follow.

In 1932, aboard his yacht the **REN-MAR**, formerly the **REOMAR III**, Bidwell with the encouragement of his wife bought the National Football League's Chicago Cardinals for $50,000. The Bidwell descendants still own the NFL team now known as the Arizona Cardinals.

Shortly before Charley Bidwell's death in 1947, the yacht was sold to Richard Kritzler of Chicago Il. Kritzler was a successful manufacturer of refrigeration equipment. He renamed the yacht The **DORIC**. The Kritzlers used the **DORIC** primarily in the Great Lakes around Lake Michigan. A newspaper report from Feb, 1947 states the Kritzler family will be returning from spending the month of March in Palm Beach. Upon their return, the **DORIC's** interior will have been done over in a French 18th century style with murals painted on many interior walls.

The **DORIC** was then sold to Edward H. Jones, a successful oilman from Texas in 1948. The yacht's name was changed to the **KASIDAH II**. The yacht was used primarily in Florida and was moored at the Sarasota Yacht Club. The Jones' had maintained a winter home in Venice, Florida.

By this point, the **KASIDAH II** was 107 feet and captained by R.S. McCallan with a crew of 7. She retained her twin 275hp diesels. A local paper commented on March 23, 1951 that "She is one of the few big yachts that have been built on the Great Lakes and brought to Florida waters". The **KASIDAH II** flew the burgee of the New York Yacht Club. In March, 1953, the yacht was again cruising Florida waters near Fort Myers. She was known as a regular visitor to the area, however she could not moor at Fort Myers due to overcrowding in the yacht basin! Jones owned the yacht until 1956 when ownership passed to his wife. She owned the yacht for two years and sold it to Jeannea Saunders.

Little is known about Jeannea or her husband Frank, who had died in 1954. A newspaper society column in 1949 mentioned that her parents were hosting a dinner party for them. The same article also mentioned that the Saunders were the owners of the yacht **JEANNEA III** in which they have cruised to Hawaii, the Orient and other lands.

In February, 1972, Mrs. Saunders donated the **KASIDAH II** to Texas A & M for use in their oceanographic fleet. The University said the yacht would be converted and used as the prime vessel for studies along the continental shelf in the Gulf of Mexico. At the time of the donation, the yacht was appraised for $175,000.

David L. Davis, President of Texas Caribbean Trading Company purchased **KASIDAH II** soon after Mrs. Saunders donated it to Texas A & M. It is likely that the University, when it realized the on-going maintenance costs of the vessel, put it up for sale.

Davis purchased the yacht because it retained much of what he called "its Roaring Twenties qualities". The mahogany paneling interior was still intact. Surprisingly, a large elegant antique vanity with mirrors was also left in place probably due to its size. Davis also discovered a secret mirrored panel which opened between the master stateroom and an adjoining cabin. Records do not indicate if the secret panel was part of the original construction.

Davis stated there were more than a dozen staterooms which is inconsistent with the original plans for the yacht. Along the way, the yacht had been changed from its original 6 stateroom layout to be able to accommodate more quarters for officers and sailors. Apparently in a mode to keep remodeling expenses under control, someone had decided to keep the old-fashioned cast iron steam radiators in place.

A safe was found in the master stateroom; according to Davis, the safe was circa 1924. That would indicate the safe was installed by Olds which is entirely plausible given the need to protect the jewelry and other possessions of the Olds family and guests.

Davis indicated that it took some effort to open the safe which apparently, due to its condition, had not been opened in many years. After finally opening it, the safe was discovered to contain several Luger shells and .38mm police shells that crumbled upon touch.

Davis had a large aquarium on one deck that was fed with fresh saltwater from a series of circulating pumps. A local workman involved with the restoration said the fresh saltwater recirculation system "…was right out of Jules Verne." When the yacht was purchased in the 1970's, the aquarium was one of the first thing to go.

By 1974, the former **REOMAR III** was in Corpus Christi, Texas. It had been purchased by a Jim ("Jimmy") Storm, a successful oil driller. The yacht would have the same captain for the next 20 years. Storm, who had died in the summer of 1991, had renamed the yacht, the **CELIKA S** after his wife, the daughter of a former President of Argentina.

The Storms kept the yacht at the Corpus Christi Marina during their years of ownership. They were reportedly very generous and often loaned the yacht out for fund-raisers by local non-profits and for tours. During the Storm's ownership of the former **REOMAR III** was the first time the purported Capone connection came up. Therefore, there is some evidence to indicate that the Capone rumor may have been initiated or embellished with Storm's ownership.

In the early 1990's, R E Olds Anderson, grandson of R.E. Olds (and father-in-law of the author), was contacted by a personal friend who thought he might have seen the **REOMAR III/CELIKA S**. Anderson described the yacht in detail from memory, having spent many years of his youth aboard the yacht, and his friend was indeed able to make identification. The friend put Anderson in touch with the owner who was anxious to sell the boat to Anderson or a museum.

After Jim Storm's death in 1991, Mel Miller purchased the **CELIKA S.** for $150,000 (nearly $273,000 in 2017 dollars). In 1992, he took the yacht up to New Orleans for the Madisonville Boat Festival from its normal mooring spot in Corpus Christi. Miller planned first to take it to the Akers-Gulf Marine Fabricators in Ingleside, Texas for a four to five month overhaul. Its electrical wiring and waste removal system were in drastic need of upgrading. It was soon determined that **CELIKA S** was to need a new steel bottom and engines...that was to be the start of her undoing. In December, 1992 the Coast Guard approved the plans for the refurbishment of the yacht.

Source: Mel Miller (taken in 1993)

At the point the boat was rediscovered by the Olds family, it was owned by a Mel Miller. Mr. Miller had owned an executive yacht charter previously but the ship had burned in a "freak dock fire" on June 12, 1991 in San Francisco. When he found the **CELIKA S**, he knew this elegant yacht was the perfect replacement for his business. Miller had been told prior to the purchase of the yacht that George H.W. Bush had been on board while he was Vice-President and Ronald Reagan, before becoming President, had also been a visitor to the yacht. None of these visits have been verified. Miller's plans were to take the **CELIKA S** into dry dock at Ingleside, Texas in late January 1993 for refurbishment. He wanted to paint the sides of the boat black versus the white the yacht had always been painted. One can only imagine the horror that Olds Anderson must have felt. Miller's plans were to take the refreshed yacht to New Orleans for executive charters. He also planned on changing the yacht's name to his mother's name. History is unclear but the name was either going to be **OLEETA** or **OLITA**.

By now the **CELIKA S** length had been extended to 110 feet from its original 100 foot length. She had undergone 2 refits, 1950 and 1975. The original Mianus diesel engines had been replaced with two Cummins diesel engines. The cruising speed of 10 knots remained unchanged. **CELIKA S** could still accommodate 12 guests.

By 1999, Miller had spent $900,000 on refurbishing the **CELIKA S**. and the job was far from done. She now needed at least another $1mm in repairs! However, Miller was out of money. Miller's mother was wealthy and had funded this indulgence but even she eventually called a halt to the restoration. Miller, who was now a private investigator in Corpus Christi, had tried to entice investors but after due diligence, each potential deal fell through. Miller was desperate and even stated to a Corpus Christi newspaper in February, 1999 that he would give the boat away for $50,000…or less. Moving the yacht to another shipyard would cost at least $30,000, a deterrent to many investors. The last correspondence to Olds Anderson in 1999 indicated the yacht would be "cut-up" in a week.

In early 2015, an individual contacted the writer and claimed the **REOMAR III** was still in the shipyard. Miller, as the last owner had died in a "hit & run" accident some years earlier. He was never able to reclaim the yacht as the storage fees had come unmanageable. The shipyard where the **REOMAR III** purportedly resided would not let anyone on the premises to inspect the hull. This individual was able to contact a friend who was employed at the shipyard who verified the hull had been cut up BUT only in the past year or two! Supposedly, the remaining teak and mahogany was removed and used for furniture.

No trace of the **REOMAR III** or its teak, mahogany or furniture was ever discovered. It is assumed the yacht is lost to history.

REOMETTA: Launched in 1928; Owned for one run

The story of the *REOMETTA* is quite interesting...and short. With the *REOMAR III*, Olds would have only one yacht for 4 years. Since his decision to close out his investment in Oldsmar, Olds no longer was spending considerable time in Florida. The style of boat he preferred in Florida, a shallow water trunk cabin cruiser, like the *REOLA II*, was no longer needed. Practically speaking, the Olds family didn't need two yachts as their summers in the 1920's were spent traveling or taking extended cruises, including a 6 month around the world cruise in 1924.

Source: Olds Family – Ed Roe
Please note that R.E. Olds is standing on the rear deck.

Before 1928, Olds owned the *REOMAR III*. It was a beautiful yacht and Olds took great pride in its design and construction. Yet, for reasons lost to history, Olds ordered the construction of another yacht. The *REOMETTA* was of a trunk cabin design, just 63 feet long with a beam of 15.5 feet. The draft was 6.3 feet, more substantial than the *REOLA II* and the *REOMAR III* but not matching the *REOMAR II*'s draft of 8.1 feet. The larger draft design would have helped ensure better stability in strong winds by reducing the center of gravity due to the ballast over the keel of the boat.

The *REOMETTA* had a small forward deck and a large sun deck at the stern. The main cabin was furnished with numerous chairs, davenports, a buffet and a writing desk. The design included four staterooms, a bathroom, a kitchen galley and engine room.

Source: Olds Family Archives – Stephens

The **REOMETTA** was powered with two 75hp. Hill Diesels from Lansing, MI. It was only natural that when it was time to design yet another yacht, Olds would turn to Hill Diesel to supply the power plant for the new yacht. Cruising speed was approximately 10 knots or 12 MPH.

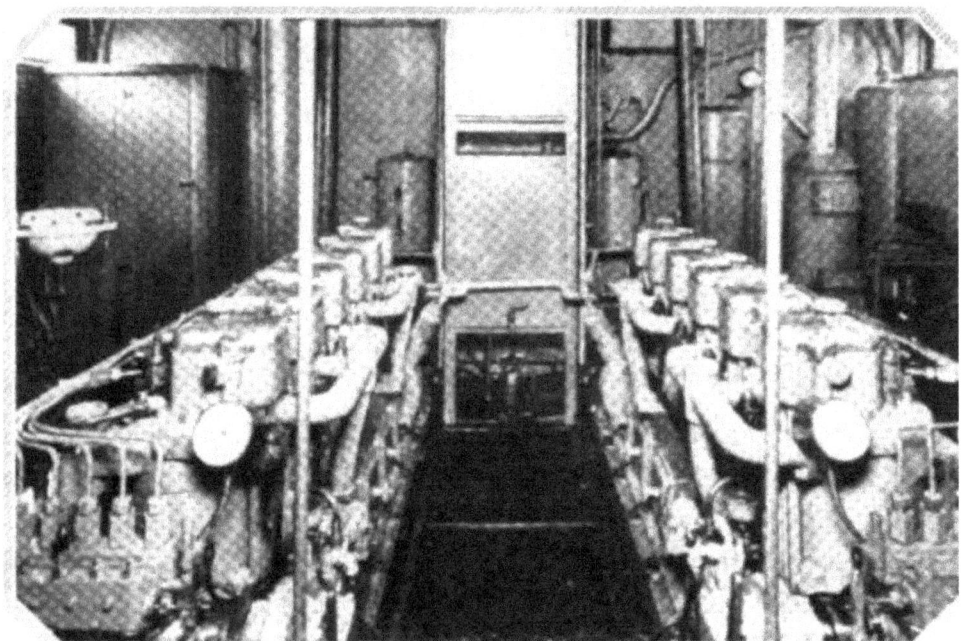
Source: Olds Family Archives - Stephens

Olds originally invested in the predecessor firm of Hills Diesel in 1924. Olds helped reorganized the newly called Hill Diesel Company in Lansing, MI in 1929. It was run by his old friend Harry Hill, who like Olds was a mechanical genius. Over the following decade, Olds' investment in Hill Diesel approached $700,000. Hill Diesel was sold to Rogers Diesel and Aircraft in 1941.

> Historical fact: *Olds had been one of the few automotive pioneers who experimented in steam, electric and gas engines. Now through his investment in Hill Diesel, he was experimenting in diesel power. Olds continue to explore the potential for diesel engines in automobiles and yachts but without much luck. In fact, Olds received a patent for an opposed piston diesel engine in November, 1937 (Patent Number: 2,099,371) which was assigned to Hill Diesel. Hill Diesel was sold to Rogers Diesel and Aircraft Co. in 1941. In 1947 Rogers Diesel was merged with Indian Motorcycle Co, another division of R.B. Rogers Company. By the early 1950's Indian Motorcycle, which had been bigger than Harley Davidson, was out of business.*

The yacht was designed and constructed in Morris Heights, NY by the New York Yacht, Launch & Engine Co. This yacht signaled the end of Olds' long relationship with yacht designer's Cox & Stevens. Why that relationship ended has been lost to history.

With the **REOMAR III** as his yacht of choice for the northern summer months, Olds was clearly looking for a different style of yacht for cruising in the shallow warm waters of Florida. **REOMETTA** at 63 feet, a beam of 15.5 feet and a draft of 6.3 feet, was quite a departure for the size of parties that Olds was used to taking on his yachts.

Interestingly, Olds only used the **REOMETTA** once! He took it for a cruise up the Hudson River after its launch and turned it in. He then began planning the construction of the larger **METTAMAR**. Why the **REOMETTA** was turned in so quickly was never recorded. Given Olds' propensity for cruising with large groups, it is likely that he realized this boat simply did not adequately fit his needs. His recent yachts were either close to or exceeded 100'. His guest list typically was 10 to 12 people. This yacht would have felt exceptionally small and crowded to him. But clearly one trip on the **REOMETTA** was enough to convince him that it wasn't suitable for his purposes.

The yacht was later sold to a Mr. Hayes of Jackson, Michigan. The **REOMETTA** was sold again and renamed the **VIRGINIA LEE**. In 1941, a local paper in the Upper Peninsula of Michigan had a story about the **HIAWATHA**, formerly the **VIRGINIA LEE**, being purchased by the Cleveland-Cliffs Iron Company to be put into service as a ferry boat between Munising and Grand Island, with occasional excursions around the island. It still had its small forward deck and the large sun deck. The yacht now carried 72 people but still had four staterooms a bathroom and a kitchen. Its diesel engines were replaced with new diesel engines capable of 220 horsepower each.

The whereabouts of the **HIAWATHA/REOMETTA** today is unknown.

The FLYING CLOUD: built 1928; owned 1928 to 1930

However, before the **METTAMAR** was constructed, Olds had contacted the Robinson Marine Construction Company of Benton Harbor, Michigan to discuss the construction of a commuter boat. The company had planned to build a series of "small lake cruisers". Olds, as it turns out, was looking for another type of boat for his Florida home. He felt this type of sedan cruiser, with its "V" bottom could be perfect for cruising Florida's lakes and rivers.

The Robinson Marine Construction Company of Benton Harbor, Michigan was started in 1926. Glenn Robinson contracted with John Hacker, noted boat designer and naval architect, to design the "small lake cruiser" that Robinson was planning to develop.

Historical fact: *John Hacker (1877-1961) had many major contributions. Among them were the invention of the "V" hull design and the floating biplane for the Wright Brothers. The "V" hull produced stunning speed at great efficiency utilizing low horsepower.*

Source: Olds Family Archives - Stephens

R.E. Olds on **THE FLYING CLOUD** on the day of its delivery in Jacksonville, FL.

Olds named his new commuter boat **THE FLYING CLOUD** after one of the popular REO car models of the day. The Flying Cloud boat was 36' in length with an 8' beam. The draft of the boat was 2 feet 6 inches; perfect for Florida coastal waters. It was planked with ½" African Mahogany. White oak was used for the keel, stem and frame.

She came with a 150hp Sterling engine and could comfortably carry 6 passengers. The Sterling engine could cruise at 28 to 39 MPH. Other engine options included: Kermath 225hp (30 to 32 MPH), Scripps V-12 (32 to 35 MPH), and a Garwood Liberty (40 to 45 MPH).

It was built with the signature Hacker "V" bottom. With its leather covered hardtop cabin roof, the boat looked every inch like an automobile limousine. As was Olds' habit, he loved to insert himself into all aspects of the design. **The FLYING CLOUD**, according to newspaper account of the day, had "a look of a smart automobile" and ..."is steered with the same ease as an auto"... Olds had requested Pullman style berths, a small galley with an ice box and a separate head, or toilet, with a very unique fold-up lavatory sink. Olds had purchased the very first Seagull and the first commuter boat!

> Historical fact: *The Flying Cloud car was an upscale car introduced in 1927 by REO. Designed by Fabio Segardi, its name established a trend for how cars were named thereafter.*

Glenn Robinson, owner of the shipbuilding company, stated in the local paper that a sister ship to **The FLYING CLOUD**, called the **NYMPH**, was almost complete and would be shipped to an "Eastern millionaire". Robinson speculated that 8 more cruisers would be built based upon existing orders. At the point **The FLYING CLOUD** was built, the Robinson Company had only been in existence for three years but had already turned out 16 cruisers generating $200,000 in revenue. Robinson employed 25 men who constructed **The FLYING CLOUD** and **NYMPH** in several weeks, according to a newspaper account of the day. Robinson had decided to build two types of cruisers: a cabin version and a sedan cruiser or commuter. Robinson had hit upon an idea to build a small power boat that could run at an acceptable speed and yet could be outfitted in a luxurious manner as was required by the market.

Robinson shipped the boat by railcar to Florida on February 11, 1928. Olds had several boats shipped by railcar as he still had that existing arrangement with a Midwest circus to use one of their railcars as needed. His grandson, Olds Anderson was 12 at the time, and remembered the delivery and subsequent trip down the St John's River well. The Olds family in their personal family archives, has film taken of the delivery and the initial trial run before proceeding to their home on South Halifax St. in Daytona Beach, Fl. There is also film footage of the family returning from an outing in **THE FLYING CLOUD**. Everyone is dressed in their finery and the women were wearing heavy coats.

Source: Olds Family Archives - Stephens

THE FLYING CLOUD underway in Daytona, FL near the Olds' home. The notation on the photograph was written by R.E. Olds Anderson, oldest grandson of the Olds'.

The ownership of The Flying Cloud is somewhat unclear. At some point in the 1930's, **THE FLYING CLOUD** was bought by a Clarence Welch of Michigan, who was told at the time of purchase that it had been Capone's boat previously. (See section on Al Capone ownership of Olds' yachts on page 40) Welch's daughter stated in a much later interview that the family used the boat in Florida in the winter and then had the boat brought to Michigan for summer use. The Welchs' maintained the boat for many years before selling it to Emmett Roche, inventor and founder of Emrola Radio, in 1949. The Emrola radio was short lived; Roche developed it and sold them out of his automotive service station. The boat was used by the family for fishing trips on Lake Michigan for many years. His son Stuart, was quoted years later that as a youth he was enlisted to be the driver for the family fishing trips. Stuart Roche recalled that **THE FLYING CLOUD** probably was last refinished in the 1960's. Roche continued the family practice of transporting the boat between Michigan and Florida, reportedly around New Port Richey. However, the boat suffered as regular maintenance and upkeep was no longer maintained. By the time of Roche's death in the 1970's, the boat was in a seriously deteriorated condition. **THE FLYING CLOUD** changed hands several more times, each new owner hoping to be the one to do the full restoration. The Flying Cloud was the first Robinson Seagull and now the last in existence. She was dangerously close to being trashed due to the enormous cost to restore her.

In 1996, Clay and Patty Thompson of Altus, Oklahoma purchased **THE FLYING CLOUD** in Lake Tahoe, NV. from Al Schinnerer of California Classic Boats. The Thompsons had been to a boat show at Lake Tahoe and discovered the boat while walking to the show. The Thompson's, who own a swimming pool construction and maintenance company, had ventured into the restoration of antique boats as a way to keep employees busy (and paid) during the winter months when pool related work was quiet.

The Thompsons are expert antique boat restorers and they brought **THE FLYING CLOUD** back from a "gray" boat to its current beautiful state.

Source: Clay and Patty Thompson

Most recently, **THE FLYING CLOUD** was owned by Martin Smith, who sadly passed away at a very young age. The boat was located in Clayton, NY as his estate attempted to sell the boat. The author was able to show **THE FLYING CLOUD** to his wife, the great granddaughter of the Olds'. She was the first descendant to see one of R.E. Olds' boats in over 60 years!

THE FLYING CLOUD was sold purportedly to someone in 2016 who was planning to transfer it to the Muskoka region of Canada.

METTAMAR: built 1930; owned 1930 to 1936

The **METTAMAR** represented a new challenge to Olds. Olds decided he wanted a yacht that could be used in both northern and southern waters. His challenge was how to design a hull that could handle the rough waters of the Great Lakes and ocean excursions plus southern coastal waters with their varying tides. Olds loved to design and order new yachts incorporating some of the most notable design or engineering changes, many of which were unique to his yachts. He was 66 years old in 1930 and his interests in life had changed. He had long since lost interest in the automobile industry, preferring to focus on real estate development and alternative business ventures (Hill Diesel, Olds Tower, Kold-Hold and philanthropy).

Source: Olds Family – Ed Roe

The **METTAMAR** was a 93 foot, twin screw cruiser similar in style to the **REOMAR III** and other yachts. In the November, 1930 edition of **Yachting** magazine, it was referred to as a power houseboat. Rather than use Cox & Stevens, who had designed five of Olds' yachts to date, Olds used The New York Yacht, Launch and Engine Company (NYYLEC) to design and build the new yacht. NYYLEC had been the builder of the Cox & Stevens designed yachts for Olds previously but, in the case of the **REOMETTA** & **METTAMAR**, he made the decision to allow NYYLEC to have the entire contract, including the design. The reason for this decision has been lost but the resulting ship was a beautiful yacht incorporating many of Olds' personal design wishes. With its length of 93 feet, the **METTAMAR** had a beam of 19 feet and a draft of 4 feet 6 inches.

"Mettamar," a 93-Foot Diesel Cruiser

Here is the latest cruiser to be built for Mr. R. E. Olds, of Lansing, Mich., several of whose former yachts have appeared in YACHTING in the past. "Mettamar" is 93 feet in length and has the appointments of a power houseboat, although she follows distinctively cruising lines. Comfort and spaciousness have been attained in the living quarters, as the reproductions of the deck saloon and the owner's double stateroom indicate. The New York Yacht, Launch and Engine Company were the designers and builders, and for power she is equipped with a pair of 6-cylinder Hill-Diesels

Photos by M. Rosenfeld

Source: Olds Family Archives - Stephens, (Yachting, November, 1930)

Source: Olds Family Archives – Stephens
Courtesy: Lansing State Journal

The September 6, 1930 issue of the Lansing State Journal carried a picture of a Reo Speed Wagon that had a newly designed diesel engine for trucks installed in it to carry the massive diesel generator engine to New York for installation in the **METTAMAR**. The article went on to state that the truck consumed less than $2 worth of fuel oil during the 955 mile trip from Lansing, MI to New York…at an average speed of 30 miles per hour! <u>With the granting of patent 2099371 for a diesel engine, Olds was the only automotive pioneer to build cars or trucks that ran on steam, electric, gasoline and diesel.</u>

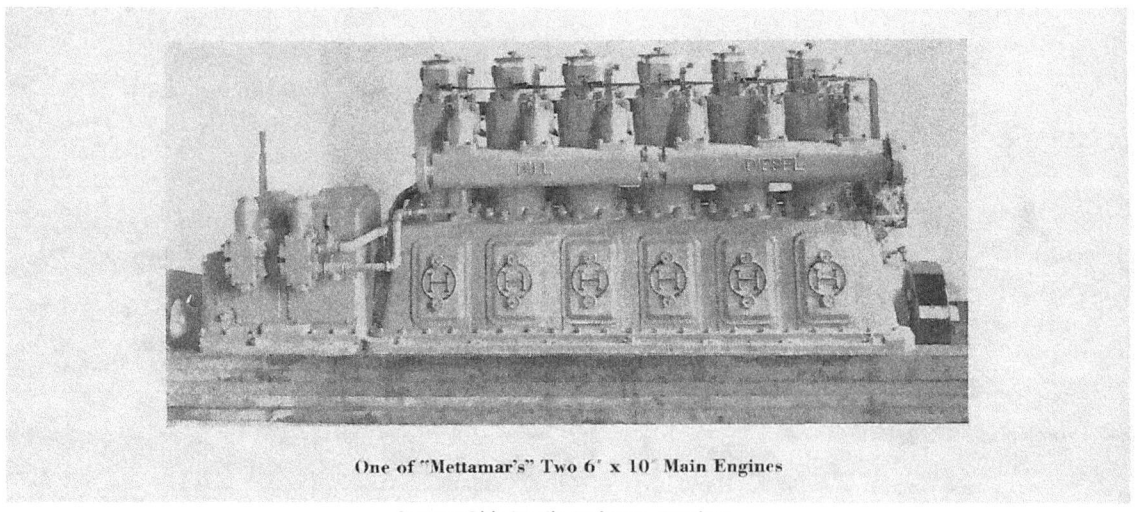

One of "Mettamar's" Two 6' x 10' Main Engines

Source: Olds Family Archives - Stephens

As Olds liked to do, he immersed himself in the development of the **METTAMAR** and her engines. The engines were dual six cylinder Hill-Diesels rated at 125 hp each. Cruising speed was between 12 and 13 miles per hour. At a gross tonnage of 115 tons, the **METTAMAR** was considerably heavier than his earlier boats used in Florida, (which were generally 70 tons or less). Given the weight, these were very reasonable cruising speeds as stated by **MotorBoating Magazine** in their February, 1931 issue.

Interestingly, when Olds commissioned the design of this ship, he intended it to be in service in both the northern and southern waters. Therefore, it had to be ocean going as well as be able to navigate in the shallower southern coastal areas with recurring tides. How Olds accomplished this was quite ingenious. Olds created a unique auxiliary power system for the **METTAMAR** to handle the cruising in Florida during the winter months. He placed a third propeller on the center line of the yacht. The power driving this propeller came from an auxiliary electric motor located in the lazarette (a small compartment typically found below the deck aft of the cockpit). Olds designed this feature so a yacht with the larger draft and more powerful engines could also be used in the shallower shoal waters in Florida at lower moderate speeds with this auxiliary engine. The controls for this electrical power plant were located on the bridge beside the controls for the regular diesel engine. The captain or helmsman thus had full control of all power options at his disposal. The power for the auxiliary engine came from a twelve kilowatt Hill-Diesel generating set. It also supplied the current for charging all the ship's batteries as well as the Frigidaire icebox, windlass, boat hoist and to power the pressure water system.

Olds had long been a proponent of electrical motors since the earliest days of his automotive endeavors. He felt the electric propulsion on the **METTAMAR** would allow his captain to maintain low to moderate speeds needed to control the yacht while in shoal waters while they were cruising in Florida.

> Historical fact: *the term lazarette comes from the Italian term, lazaretto or possibly Lazarus from the Bible. In sailing times, infectious crew or the bodies of deceased prominent passengers were stored here. Deceased "less" prominent passengers and crew were thrown overboard.*

Olds himself designed the accommodations for the yacht. He often traveled with large groups as noted before. As guests of the Olds', days were not totally calm and relaxing. Events were planned and activities scheduled through the day, even on-board the ship! However, Olds took great steps to ensure guest accommodations were comfortable and extremely livable, when they had time to go to their quarters! Separate berths or beds for up to nine people were provided. There were also two bathrooms. R.E. & Metta Olds had a double stateroom for their use. Pressurized water systems for both salt and fresh water were provided. The launch for the Olds' was equipped with a Van Blerck engine.

> Historical fact: *Before 1910, Van Blerck worked with Henry Ford on an early prototype of a Model T engine. Beginning around 1910, Van Blerck started building marine engines and they soon had a reputation of reliability*

and being long lasting. At one point, he was also associated with Ross Judson and Continental Motors where they offered a Continental-Van Blerck engine.

The dining room was placed in the forward deckhouse. The specially designed dining table seated ten people comfortably. The after house was 21 feet by 12 feet 6 inches and was a large comfortable interior living space. Of course, Olds had installed an electric player piano as well as a Victrola and the most modern radio. Due to the fact that this yacht was primarily in warmer waters, the yacht has a large open air space with a sun cover for the guests to relax and enjoy the sights.

All furniture and decorations were selected by Olds from suggestions made by the interior design firm.

Source: Olds Family Archives - Stephens

A typical Olds family gathering on the **METTAMAR**. Metta Olds, wife of R.E. Olds, third from the left, is seated wearing a white dress.

Olds owned the **METTAMAR** until 1936 at which time it was sold to Frances C. Griscom of Philadelphia. While Olds never stated his reasons for selling the **METTAMAR**, he was 72 in 1936 and certainly keeping a slower pace of life. Also, since he had severed his ties with The REO Motor Car Company earlier, he was no longer receiving the significant dividends of those earlier years. Olds' personal income during this time was derived from his bonds and mortgage holdings. Correspondence from Olds to his daughters at the time asked them to curtail their expenditures since they all "needed to live within their means" and not force him to liquidate his bonds. Olds was providing an allowance or income to many family members, most notably his daughters and their families. In the end, the **METTAMAR** was probably sold due to Olds' advancing old age and his financial conservatism. He still certainly had the capital, if not the income flow, to enjoy both yachts and more!

Miss Griscom was well known as the daughter of shipping magnate Clement Griscom but she was also quite accomplished in her own right. She was the 1900 U.S. Women's Amateur golf champion, winning at Shinnecock Hills Golf Club in Southampton, Long Island. During her ownership, the society pages up and down the east coast mentioned the visits of the **METTAMAR** and her frequent tarpon fishing trips in Florida.

> Historical fact: *Clement Griscom was the President of the International Mercantile Marine Company (IMM) formed in conjunction with J.P. Morgan in 1902 in an effort to build an international shipping conglomerate of multiple shipping and passenger lines. Griscom continued as President of IMM until 1904 until he resigned and assumed the role of Chairman of the Board of Directors. IMM owned, among its many holdings, the White Star Line, which operated the **Titanic**. Griscom died a few months after the Titanic disaster.*

The **METTAMAR** was sold by Frances Griscom in 1939 to Barbara Hutton, heiress to the Woolworth family fortune. Ownership of the **METTAMAR** remained with Hutton until 1942 when the Navy commandeered her for duty in World War II as a training ship and patrol boat off the coast of New England. The **METTAMAR** was sent to Fyfe's Shipyard in Glenwood Landing, Long Island, NY to be refitted for war duty. She was lengthened to 105 feet and refitted with new engines. Known as **USS-YP 521**, she served admirably until the war's end.

Hutton went on to own other yachts, most notably the 240 foot yacht named **VANADIS**. It was supposedly given to her on her 18th birthday! Today the yacht **VANADIS** is at anchor in Stockholm and had been converted to a 60 room hotel. Her present name is the **Lady Hutton**.

> Historical fact: *Barbara Hutton was the granddaughter of F.W. Woolworth and was considered to be the "original poor little rich girl". She was fabulously wealthy and had little regard for other people or her own reputation. Her lavish lifestyle and unfortunate diet of drugs and alcohol resulted in her early death at the age of 66 and the wasting of the family fortune. She reputedly had $3,500 to her name at the time of her death.*

After the war in 1946, the **METTAMAR** was sold to a H.E. Greist of Noroton, Connecticut for $9,010 by the War Shipping Administration, which was charged with the responsibility of disposing of all the personal yachts commandeered for the war effort. The yacht was renamed as the **HAROLYN**. In 1963, the yacht was renamed the **METTAMAR** and owned by a John Huffman of Jacksonville, FL.

By the early 1980's, the **METTAMAR** was owned by a John Alvenus of Crystal River, Fl. The local papers record the yacht being towed into Kings Bay at Crystal River, Florida on March 20, 1981. By late 1981, the yacht was tied up in Tarpon Springs, Florida for a period of time. According to the local paper, two men are claiming ownership but neither could document their claims.

Source: Olds Family Archives - Stephens

By 1982, the yacht was now owned by a Wes Doolen who was moving it to the Sea Ranch subdivision in Hudson, FL to undergo a remodeling at his shipyard. Doolen's plan, according to the newspaper, was to outfit the boat over a few years, staff it with an all-woman crew and head up the Amazon River! The above picture shows an old and weary **METTAMAR** being towed into Hudson, Fl. Telling of the yachts' fate, it ran aground and had to be towed into its new mooring location.

In August, 1981 a regional newspaper in Florida ran an article on the **METTAMAR's** mysterious past. One article stated that Joseph P. Kennedy Sr. built it. The fact that no mention of Olds, or the fact he built it, is evidence of poor journalistic research. The same is true of the rumor that the **METTAMAR** was used during the Yalta Conference on the Black Sea during World War II. Even the most elementary of research effort would have shown that neither of these rumors could possibly be true. The Kennedy estate and the Naval Historical Center have stated in the past that they know of no connection to the **METTAMAR**.

The last known sighting of the **METTAMAR** was in Hudson, Florida in the 1980's as mentioned above. Her current whereabouts are unknown.

REOMAR IV: built 1926; owned by Olds from 1931 to 1942

Source: Olds Family Archives - Stephens

The **REOMAR IV** was a stunning ship. Designed and built by the Defoe Boat and Motor Works, Bay City, Michigan in 1926 originally for Logan Thomson, a Michigan lumber magnate, it was originally named the **SYLVIA IV**. The yacht had been sold to Ross Judson, retired president of Continental Motors Corp. On May 12, 1931, Charles Ross, a yacht broker, arranged the sale of the **SYLVIA IV** to Olds for $75,000 (nearly $1.2 million in 2018) in cash and the exchange of the **REOMAR III**. Olds also bought the large boathouse in Round Lake, Charlevoix from Thompson which was built to house the yacht. Ross then sold the **REOMAR III** to former Michigan governor, Alex J. Groesbeck later that summer.

Ross Judson was sued by Charles Ross in November, 1931 for failure to pay a commission of the sale of the **SYLVIA IV**. Charles Ross was seeking damages of $10,500 as payment for the commission on the sale of the **SYLVIA IV** to Olds. Olds was not a party to this lawsuit.

Judson was already dealing with another lawsuit for $225,000 from a 22 year old divorcee claiming a "breach of promise" for marriage. However, Mr. Judson, separated from his wife, was not divorced nor claimed to be. Both Judson's and the divorcee's attorney were quoted in a local paper as laughing at her claim of a "breach of promise".

Historical fact: *Ross Judson is a name almost lost to history. His company played an integral part in the development of the American automobile industry. Judson, a gifted engineer, started an automotive engine business in Detroit in 1903. His partner (and brother-in-law) displayed their first engine in 1903 at the Chicago*

Automobile Show. From their start of 100 engines in 1905, to 1,000 engines for Studebaker in 1906, they rapidly grew making 10,000 engines for Hudson in 1910. The company, now called Continental Motors, made engines for most of the auto companies including truck engines for REO. The company branched out into agricultural and aviation engines but an ill-fated attempt at a Continental branded car nearly bankrupted the company. The company survived to the 1960's and was later best known for supplying engines for the early Jeeps and Checker cabs. Judson and his brother-in-law were significant pioneers in the American automotive industry but are rarely recognized today.

Also of historical interest is the history of Witcomb L. Judson, father of Ross W. Judson. The elder Judson was a noted inventor. His earliest inventions were for a pneumatic street railway system starting in 1888 and 1889. His concept was to suspend pistons beneath the railcar. His idea of a pneumatic railway was not the first; similar efforts had failed, but Judson was able to create a demonstration line in 1890 in Washington, D.C. The line ran along the current day Georgia Avenue for only a few weeks when technical problems shut it down as well. The streetcar was sold to a local streetcar firm and electrified for future use. However, Whitcomb Judson is best known for the invention of the "zipper" or known as the "clasp-locker" in his day. His invention was received to great reviews at the Chicago World's Fair in 1893 and relieved the effort associated with fastening high button boots. In 1923, B.F. Goodrich Company installed these fasteners in the rubber galoshes and called the new design "Zippers" thus forever changing the name of the product forever.

The **SYLVIA IV** was involved in a very unusual accident in Charlevoix in 1928 when owned by Thomson. Entering into the channel leading into the harbor, the **SYLVIA IV** signaled for the bridge to open. It was a very dark night. From where the bridge-house was located, it was not possible to see down the channel to Lake Michigan due to a building and the bend in the channel. The bridge tender, a man of great standing for his sense of duty, assumed the small sailboat in the channel was the vessel that had given the signal. As he watched the sailboat slide into Round Lake, he initiated steps to close the bridge. The bridge-tender had totally missed the **SYLVIA IV**! She was proceeding under full power as he watched the yacht crash into the bridge. **SYLVIA IV** lost her mast, caved in the pilothouse and sent the pilothouse windows crashing into the decks. According to reports of the day, the collision could be heard all over Charlevoix as could the screams of the women on board. Thomson himself was gracious and accepting that it was truly an accident. The yacht was able to operate under its own power and soon returned to the Defoe shipyard in Bay City for repairs.

Interestingly, Olds once again showed his creative engineering side when presented with a problem. Northern Michigan winters are known for their cold weather and brutal winds. Yachts owners were typically faced with a difficult financial choice during northern winters: haul their boats out if possible, transfer them to warmer climates or hire crew to be vigilant and constantly watch and chip away accumulated ice from around their yacht. Olds realized there was a natural spring by the boat house. According to his grandson, R E Olds Anderson, Olds diverted the flow from the spring into the boat house well and thus created one of the first systems now known in modern times as a bubbling system. This natural flow was enough to ensure that the water wouldn't freeze! This boathouse structure is still in existence today in Charlevoix but it has been converted to condos.

The **REOMAR IV** was a twin screw diesel, a highly efficient engine for its day. It had a plumb bow, much like the Titanic, which was intended to make the boat more efficient by slicing smoothly through the water. Angled bows will force the water under the boat which requires more energy to displace the water already there. She also had a fantail stern.

Her dimensions were: Length Overall 133 feet; the beam is 18.6 feet. and the draft is 6 feet. The weight of the yacht is 155 gross tons; she was powered with twin diesels each engine rated at 300HP. Top speed was 11 knots. The engines were placed in the forward section of the ship as the current thinking of naval architects of the day believed that this configuration gave the ship more stability, particularly on the high seas. Reportedly, the propeller drive shafts ran the length of the vessel.

Source: Olds Family Archives - Stephens

The **REOMAR IV** engine room

Source: Olds Family Archives - Stephens

The **REOMAR IV** underway leaving Charlevoix, Michigan.

REOMAR IV was intended for a crew of between 12 and 14 but was the case with Olds, the yacht operated with far fewer with the typical number being 8 or 9. The typical crew was the Captain, officer, bosun, two deck hands, mess boy, engineer and an assistant and a chef.

A letter from a member of the crew is fascinating in its rich detail of life aboard the **REOMAR IV**. Olds was a fan of movies so during the cruises, if they came upon a town or harbor, Olds would drop a crew's tender over the side so some of the crew could row into town and check what movie was playing. If the movie did not suit Olds, "up went the anchor and on to the next town or harbor."

Olds did not particularly like cruising in rough weather, which is one reason why he loved his vacation home on Lake Charlevoix. After one made it into Round (then called Pine) Lake, the protected waters of Lake Charlevoix, awaited the yachtsman.

One episode was in particular quite entertaining. The yacht was approaching Charlevoix in high seas and strong winds. The Captain called for all spare crew to assemble on the deck just outside where the player piano was located just in case it broke loose. The crew was extremely concerned that if the player piano broke loose that they could never hold it in place. Meanwhile, in the after cabin, according to the crew member: *"Mrs. Olds was in the after cabin in a (sic) easy chair having the time of her life. Her chair would slide across the carpet and she would put her foot up to stop it at the wall. Than it would slide back across to the other side. We were really rolling."* Meanwhile Olds and some of his guests had congregated in the pilot house…probably the worst place one could be in a rolling sea as the higher one is on a yacht, the greater the swing. One of the women passengers in the pilot house was on her knees convinced her end was near as she was praying "for all she was worth." The crew member ended by saying that a number of passengers "had taken up station by the numerous toilets in the ship. Some of these wished they had died or could die." The yacht eventually tried to enter the channel at Charlevoix but the strong winds were blowing the 133 foot yacht sideways as she attempt to enter the port. The Captain made 3 attempts, each time turning around to avoid a potential problem. She successfully cleared the channel on the 4th attempt, much to the relief of the sick passengers.

Source: Olds Family Archives - Stephens

The **REOMAR IV** lounge

The crew member remembered this job with affection. It was his first real job and the money earned allowed him to pursue his education as a teacher. He started on the *REOMAR IV* in the spring of 1936. He stated he did not leave the ship more than 4 or five times that summer. He started as a mess boy keeping the crew's quarters clean. He made 80 cents an hour but received free room, board and clothing.

On August 14, 1936, The *REOMAR IV* made headlines for a much more important reason. Two boys, Leonard Luck and George Flagler, from Chicago were lost in Lake Michigan.

R. E. Olds' Yacht Rescues Youths

Two Chicago boys who spent all Sunday night clinging to an overturned boat five miles out in Lake Michigan near Holland were rescued Monday morning by the Reomar IV, private yacht owned by R. E. Olds of Lansing, according to word received here by Mr. Olds.

The yacht located the boys, Leonard Luck and George Flagler, five miles out in the lake and 11 miles from Holland. No Lansing residents were aboard Mr. Old's yacht when the rescue was made.

Source: Lansing State Journal (August 14, 1936)

Their boat had capsized and they had drifted five miles out into Lake Michigan off Holland. The Great Lakes had been in the midst of a sweltering heat wave that summer and the boys were seeking relief from the heat. Unfortunately, they ended up spending the night in the water clinging to their overturned boat until they were rescued on Monday by the **REOMAR IV**. The boys were fine and returned to their parents later that day. Luck was, indeed, with them.

REOMAR IV was well known on the Great Lakes. It was usually a front page event when the yacht moored in a city. The Traverse City Record-Eagle of August 22, 1938 announced with a front page spread that Olds had brought a party from St. Louis to visit Glen Lake and the surrounding area. Next to the Olds announcement was an article that the largest trout of the year had been caught: 33 pounds, 40 ½" in length and a girth of 26 ¾ inches! But that fish paled in comparison to the record trout of 43 pounds caught the previous year!

The following photograph of R.E. & Metta Olds was taken in 1938 on the **REOMAR IV** at Put-it-Bay, Ohio. The view is of Perry's Monument on South Bass Island.

Source: Olds Family Archives - Stephens

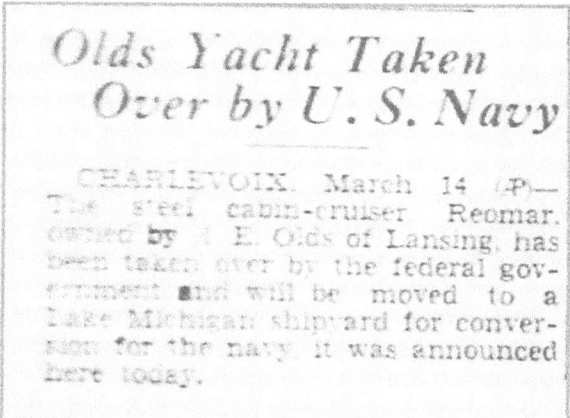

Source: Olds Family Archives - Stephens

World War II changed everything and significantly impacted the wealthy and their yachting endeavors. Everyone was expected to sacrifice for the war effort. All gave according to their means. The **REOMAR IV** in March 12, 1942 was taken over by the US government to be converted to use by the US Navy. The yacht was converted to naval wartime use by the Sturgeon Bay Shipbuilding & Drydock Co. of Sturgeon Bay, Wisconsin. The vessel was commissioned on September 28, 1942. She was renamed the USS Ability. Lt. (jg) Lloyd R. Walker was the first to command her. She was refitted with an undetermined number of 20mm mounts and three .50 caliber machine guns. The existing twin diesel engines were replaced with three 300 Cooper Bessemer's 8-G6m, two shafts. Under the Navy configuration, she had a cruising range of 1,700 nautical miles at 13 to 14 knots.

The US government took the **REOMAR IV** under its rights from the Fifth Amendment of the US Constitution. The government is granted the power to take private property for public use, however, the government must pay "just" compensation to the former owner of the property being taken. We do not know how much Olds received for the yacht.

Olds' desire for the **REOMAR IV** was to leave it to the family according to his notes, especially his grandchildren. He made no mention of how he was contemplating this planned transaction nor if funds would be provided. Perhaps it was just a hopeful aspiration. Nonetheless, the war use of the **REOMAR IV** in World War Two and changing economic times dictated a different direction as the grandchildren all pursued their own interests. The Olds daughters, Gladys Anderson and Bernice Roe, continued the family love of boating for a period of time. Gladys owned the **METTAMAR II** for a few years but her son R E Olds Anderson preferred flying. Her daughter Peggy and husband Phil Fouke were not boaters. The Roe side of the family were more involved in boating. According to Olds' great grandson Ed Roe Jr., Bernice owned a 34 foot Chris Craft cruiser (named **ROEBOAT**) and a 48 foot Chris Craft cruiser (named **ARROE II**) in the 1950's. Bernice's oldest son, Edward Olds Roe Sr., owned a 42 foot Uniflite, named **RAMBLIN ROES** in the 1960's according to his son, Thomas Roe. The youngest child of Bernice and Clarence Roe, Armin "Doc" Roe, pursued boating most of his life owning trawlers. His first boat was the **ARROE**.

Source: Olds Family Archives - Stephens

It is hard to imagine this is the same ship as the **REOMAR IV**.

After the normal shakedown and working out the kinks, the **USS ABILITY** was ordered to report to the Commander, Eastern Sea Frontier for shore patrol duty until early 1943. From March, 1943 to September, 1944 **USS ABILITY** was assigned to the Fleet Sound School in Key West, Florida. For the next year, **USS ABILITY** participated in antisubmarine warfare training exercises and handled harbor guard duties.

The **USS ABILITY** was decommissioned on September 29, 1944; she was placed as an "in service" status for duty as a naval reserve training ship at Thompkinsville, NY. Then she was placed out of service in September 19, 1945. On October 1, 1945, she was struck from the Navy Register. Later, on May 18, 1946, the former **USS ABILITY** was transferred to the Maritime Commission for disposal.

The following was a letter of appreciation received by Olds for his war contributions:

> COMMANDANT
> NINTH NAVAL DISTRICT
> GREAT LAKES, ILLINOIS
>
> 20 May 1947
>
> Mr. R. E. Olds
> Capitol National Bank Building
> Lansing, Michigan.
>
> Dear Mr. Olds:
>
> It gives me great pleasure to forward you, on behalf of the Secretary of the Navy, the World War II Yacht Owner's Certificate. It is awarded to you in grateful recognition for having made available the yacht REOMAR IV to the Navy at a time when such ships were critically needed in the defense of our country.
>
> As the USS ABILITY (PYc 28), a commissioned ship in the United States Navy, the REOMAR IV's log testifies to her faithful service. Her gallant record is a tribute to the generosity and patriotism of her owner.
>
> This certificate entitles you to fly the enclosed Naval Reserve Yacht Owner's Distinguishing Pennant not only aboard the REOMAR IV, but on any craft you may own, or sail under charter.
>
> May I add my own appreciation for your contribution to national defense.
>
> Sincerely yours,
>
> G. D. MURRAY
> Vice Admiral, U. S. Navy

Source: Olds Family Archives - Stephens

Interestingly, while the war effort took large yachts out of the hands of their owners, the advent of a new aggressive tax structure had a much greater impact on the large yachts. Few people could justify the financial impact of the new tax law against large yachts. After World War II ended, it was rare for many years to see a new yacht over 45 feet.

After the war, Olds had the opportunity to reclaim the former **REOMAR IV** but her beautiful teaks decks had been stripped and many of the interior features that Olds loved were long gone. Add on the luxury tax imposed by the government and his age (81) and even Olds realized that his love of large yachts were a thing of the past.

In the July, 1946 issue of Motor Boating, it was reported that the **REOMAR IV** (now 133 feet long) was sold to John Victor Carter of Cristobal, Canal Zone for $13,131.30. Motor Boating commented that "it sounds as if 13 must have been his lucky number". This sale undoubtedly was the start of the family rumor that the yacht ended up in the banana trade. Gladys Olds Anderson was interviewed by a local paper in 1964 on the occasion of R.E. Olds' 100th anniversary of his birth and she was quoted as stating the yacht was "engaged in the Central America banana trade". The current existence of the **REOMAR IV** is unknown.

Source: Olds Family Archives - Stephens

R.E. Olds' personal notes on his yachting experiences indicated there was another yacht he purchased in 1939. She was the **NAYADA** and was owned by C. M. Greiner of Springfield, Ohio. **NAYADA** was built in 1928 by the New York Yacht, Launch & Engine Company (NYYL&E) of Morris Heights, NY. At 70 feet length, she was 75 gross tons. The yacht was powered by two 4 cylinder 20th Century gas engines. The beam and draft is unknown.

Olds purchased the boat with the intent of keeping her in Florida. There are few details about the yacht or his ownership. Olds had a long familiarity with the NYYL&E boat building company because they had built several other yachts for him but we don't even know when Olds sold this yacht. It could be that the yacht was taken for the war effort but detailed research has not revealed any further details. There is just this one picture in the family archives. The only mention of **NAYADA** is in the July, 1946 issue of Motor Boating where the sale of the **NAYADA** from Captain Peter Nilsen to E. W. Reed of Louisville, KY. The new owner intended to keep the yacht in Florida.

> **Historical fact**: *C. M. Greiner was the owner of The Buffalo – Springfield Roller Company, which made a line of road making and road rollers. The company provided equipment for the efforts during World War I. In 1922, a related company, Springfield Motor Sweeper Company, invented a new type of street sweeper that utilized rotary side brooms and a narrow pick-up broom. Built on an automobile chassis, it had a series of handles that operated the various brooms. It reminds one of a Rube Goldberg-esque type of machine but actually was a precursor of today's street sweepers.*

CAPTAIN ALFRED BROW:

Source: Olds Family Archives - Stephens

R.E. Olds (left) with Captain Brow (center). The gentleman on the right is unknown.

This gentleman deserves his own section. Captain Alfred Brow had been hired by Olds to be the captain of his yachts around the mid-1920's; he would stay with Olds for the next 25 years. Brow was a trusted employee and friend of Olds. Olds was very loyal to his employees as well.

Captain Alfred Brow was born October 6, 1894 in Grosse Ile, Michigan. According the 1900 US Census, Brow, at the age of 6, was living at home and was a student. By the 1910 US Census, Brow had moved in with his sister, Elizabeth and her husband August Polaska. He was living in Monguagon Township in Wayne County, near Detroit. Monguagon Township is no longer in existence.

In June, 1917, Alfred Brow filed his draft Registration Card due to World War I. He was still living with his sister and brother-in-law. By now he was employed by R.E. Olds as an *"Auto Truck Driver and Mechanic"*. Most likely, he was employed at Elbamar, Olds estate on Grosse Ile. Elbamar was a working farm and testing ground for many of Olds' inventions.

By 1920, Brow was now 25 years old, single and lodging in a rooming house on E. Elizabeth St. in Detroit. Brow was employed at a clerk in a ship yard.

Bernice Olds Roe, R.E. & Metta Olds' daughter, told her grandson, Thomas Roe, that R.E. Olds had experienced problems with his different captains. Brow had worked and spent some time on the Olds' yachts and was a familiar figure to Olds. Olds approached Brow in the late 1920's and offered to pay for the captain's training if Brow would be interested in becoming Olds' captain. By the 1930 US Census, Brow, at 35, was now married with 2 small children and living in Charlevoix, MI. He was R.E. Olds' private Captain for his yachts and would remain in his employment until the early 1950's.

In 1942, Brow again registered for the draft for World War II. He was 47 years old living at 207 Belvedere Ave. in Charlevoix, MI, with his wife and three daughters. Interestingly the Brow family lived at the boat house for the **REOMAR IV**. Brow's compensation included free housing at the Olds family boat house. Brow was gone for long periods of time as the Olds yachts frequently were in the South and being used by family and friends. Olds had purchased the boat house from Logan Thomson when he bought the 133 foot **SYLVIA IV**. (see photograph of the boathouse and yacht in Chapter 6) Today the boat house has been converted into condominiums.

Once World War II was over and the **REOMAR IV** was not coming "home", Brow opened the Brow Marina and speculated in local real estate. With the returning solders and discretionary income increasing, resort towns like Charlevoix were showing signs of growth as families were looking for an outdoor recreational lifestyle.

Captain Brow continued to run the marina he owned since 1945 on Belvedere Ave. in Charlevoix, Michigan. He sold his interest in the marina to a group of local summer residents in 1962. He continued to invest in local real estate and also built furniture. The Olds family still has two large multi-drawer cabinets made by Captain Brow out of marine plywood.

As mentioned previously, Olds was very generous with his employees, friends and family. He often would finance their business or investments. Olds, in November, 1949, financed Brow's purchase of 4 lots in Block 20, called Newman's Addition in Charlevoix, MI. The purchase price for the land was $15,000. Olds financed it at 4%. The balance was due upon Olds' death.

Captain Brow died June 1, 1970 in Charlevoix, MI. He was 75 years old at the time of his passing.

AL CAPONE

Over the years, there have been rumors circulating that two of R.E. Olds' yacht were owned by Al Capone. The rumors are related specifically to the former **REOMAR III** and **THE FLYING**

CLOUD, the Robinson Seagull commuter owned by Olds. An Ambassador Charters brochure from 1990 on the *IONA* (temporary name of the *CELIKA S*, the former *REOMAR III*) stated the vessel "is rich in history...reportedly owned by Al Capone in the 1930's..." There are numerous newspaper accounts for both the *REOMAR III* and *THE FLYING CLOUD* which refer to Capone's supposed ownership.

According to the Olds family, R.E Olds was a religious man who did not tolerate liquor or smoking. He certainly never would have entered into a transaction with someone with such a dubious reputation. Olds was a man of action and sometimes impetuous decisions, especially when it came to his yachts. He often would receive a new yacht while working on the design of its replacement. As a result, he typically traded the old yacht in as part of the transfer of consideration for the next yacht he was building. Trading assets, like hotels, real estate and yachts, was something he learned from his father and an activity he engaged in with some regularity over his lifetime.

The standard version goes that R.E. Olds sold the *REOMAR III* and *THE FLYING CLOUD* to a broker who then sold them to Capone.

The question of whether Capone actually owned these yachts is a matter of conjecture since gangsters did not typically record assets in their names for a variety of reasons, the most significant of which was to avoid tax authorities or opposing lawyers. It was typical for a "friend of a friend" to own the gangsters real estate or yachts. There are no existing pictures of Capone in the former *REOMAR III*.

The truth is that Capone could not have owned the *REOMAR III*. Olds owned it until 1931 when it was sold as part of the *REOMAR IV* transaction. It was then sold to former Michigan Governor Groesbeck who owned it for almost 2 years. Then it was sold to Charley Bidwell in 1932 and later passed to his wife, Mary Bidwell, who sold the yacht in 1947. The ownership of the *REOMAR III* is well documented. Capone was sent to prison on May 24, 1932 for federal tax evasion while Groesbeck still owned the yacht. Capone remained in prison until November 16, 1939 and was released where he remained in Florida riddled with disease (syphilis) until his death on January 25, 1947.

While the *REOMAR III* was sold in 1932 shortly after *THE FLYING CLOUD*, could *THE FLYING CLOUD* be the yacht everyone assumed that Capone had bought? Olds owned *THE FLYING CLOUD* from 1928 to 1930. Capone had been in prison from May 18, 1929 to March 17, 1930 for carrying a concealed weapon and was again in prison as mentioned above from May, 1932 to 1939. Capone's usage of the boat would have to be between March, 1930 and May, 1932. This was a time where Capone faced numerous charges for vagrancy in Miami and Chicago as well as a contempt of court charge. In addition, he was a man under considerable scrutiny, also for his mob activities, and would have found it difficult to find time to go boating. There are no known confirmed pictures of Capone in *THE FLYING CLOUD*.

In addition, there is no direct link showing Capone's ownership of **THE FLYING CLOUD**. If Capone had any involvement with this boat, it probably was through an intermediary and he would have had little time to actually use the boat from early 1930 to May 1932.

Another source, Mario Gomes of the **Al Capone Museum** online, also indicated that none of Capone's expense papers which the court required for the IRS showed ownership or expenses associated with these yachts. An IRS listing of Capone's expenses from 1924 to 1929 do list expenditures associated with a cabin cruiser and a smaller vessel but these expenses would have preceded any potential ownership of **THE FLYING CLOUD**. The papers do indicate a lavish and social lifestyle from 1930 to the end of 1931, however!

The History Channel contacted author and his wife some years ago when preparing a documentary about Capone. Again, no direct connections to the ownership of the yachts were provided but it made for interesting entertainment.

There is allegedly a photo of Capone and his son in **THE FLYING CLOUD** but unfortunately it is not a close enough shot to say with certainty it was Capone. It has been stated that the young boy in the picture is the son of Al Capone, Albert "Sonny" Capone. Debbie (Olds) Anderson Stephens, wife of the author, believes the young boy in the photo could be her father, who was two years older than Sonny, but admits the picture is difficult to clearly ascertain if it truly is her father. Until more conclusive evidence comes forth, it will most certainly remain an interesting topic of discussion and debate!

Being in a boat that's moving through the water, it's so clear. Everything falls into place in terms of what's important and what's not.

James Taylor

CHAPTER FOUR

The Final Years: 1941 to 1950

Rivers know this: There is no hurry. We shall get there some day.

Winnie the Pooh

During World War II, Olds had given up his beloved **REOMAR IV** in 1942 for the war effort. Like many of the wealthier families of the day, their large homes, as well as second homes, were closed up and secured for the duration of the war. Gas rationing was a reality and maintaining several homes was looked down upon as being unpatriotic and wasteful for the war effort.

So, the Olds' closed up their Florida home in Daytona Beach, FL and returned to their home on South Washington St. in Lansing, Michigan. They never returned to their Florida home. Their eldest daughter, Gladys Olds Anderson, closed her large home, Woldumar, on the Grand River and moved to Park Avenue on New York City. Their other daughter, Bernice Roe, stayed mostly in Lansing with her family.

Historical fact: *Fulgencio Batista, the deposed dictator of Cuba was the Olds' neighbor in Daytona Beach, Fl*

In 1941, Olds closed up Oldswoode, his 17 room log lodge, and moved to a cottage in Charlevoix. This cottage was within the village limits and faced Lake Michigan, rather than Pine (now called Round) Lake or Lake Charlevoix. The **REOMAR IV** was not commissioned for the summer season. Rather, according to a local paper, the Olds' used a new cruiser for the summer. Interesting, Olds called the cruiser the **MARY ANN**, the same name as his first steam boat that he built back in 1882.

However, the situation with Bernice was more complex due to her complications with tuberculosis. Bernice was able, for medical reasons, to obtain extra gas so she could go to their summer home in Charlevoix, Michigan for a few of the summer months. According to her daughter, Bernice "Bunny" Roe Smith, living in Charlevoix was not easy stemming from anxiety caused by the concerns that the Germans might have their minds set on bombing the Straits of Mackinac.

There was a tradeoff for Bernice and her family to enjoy a few months up north at the family cottage. Oil to heat Bernice's house in the country was so scarce that they moved into the Hotel Olds in downtown Lansing. R.E. Olds owned the hotel and it was managed by Bruce Anderson, Gladys Olds Anderson's former husband. According to Bunny, the family ate all their meals at the hotel, an experience she found very distasteful.

> Historical fact: *Gladys and Bruce Anderson built a large house southwest of Lansing, on the Grand River, which they named Woldumar (utilizing the old English spelling for Olds). After R.E. and Metta Olds passed, Gladys moved into their former home on 720 S. Washington in Lansing. Bernice and her husband, Clarence Roe, moved into Woldumar and renamed it Woldenroe. The home eventually became a restaurant before burning down. Today all that remains is ruins.*

After the war when the yachts were offered back to their owners, the environment for yachting had changed, not to mention the attitude toward yachting. The government was hungry for tax money to pay for the war and luxury yachts were assessed a special tax accordingly.

By the end of the 1920's, nearly all luxury, retail or special excise taxes imposed as part of World War I had been repealed. This included an annual use tax on yachts based upon length. These taxes had help fund the war effort but the end of the "war to end all wars" meant these special taxes could be eliminated.

However by 1932, the US government's deficit had grown and clearly a need to balance the budget had to be addressed. The Revenue Act of 1932, signed by President Herbert Hoover, raised individual tax rates significantly. Income taxes rates, at the highest level, rose from 25% to 63% (as the result of a special surtax). In addition, the estate tax rate was doubled and corporate tax rates went from 12% to 13 ¾ %.

Special excise taxes were imposed as part of an effort to balance the budget. Consumer disposable goods and luxury items were hit with significant excise taxes. A retail excise tax of 10% was levied on all boats costing more than $100,000. Retail excise taxes on consumer goods were also implemented up to 20%. Many of these so-called "luxury" taxes were not eliminated until the mid-1960's and a few, such as a telephone usage tax, remained into the late 1990's. An annual use tax on all pleasure boats, not just luxury yachts, of $10 to $200 was also implemented during The Revenue Act of 1932.

Olds had long since decided that his age, the cost of yacht ownership and the unfriendly tax on yachts made further luxury yachting a thing of the past. But he was not to be done with yachting. Olds simply downsized and adjusted. During this postwar period, Olds' correspondence with his daughter, Gladys, indicated a concern over the spending habits of his two daughters. While Olds had enough money for his or several lifetimes, he nonetheless expressed continued concerns to his daughters about their extravagant (to him) lifestyles. Many previous biographers, and friends, had expressed the opinion that Olds had a fear of being poor again. Some of the harder lessons of life had stayed with him throughout his life. Yet his sense of generosity never wavered. The long list of beneficiaries from his estate is astonishing.

From 1943 to 1947, Olds didn't own a boat. It was the longest period he had gone without a boat of some kind. 1923 was the only other time he had not had some kind of large yacht. After World War II ended, Olds again resumed his habit of having multiple boats under construction or in the design stage. In the last three years of his life, he had three yachts constructed. Two of the three came in 1950, the year that he died!

These yachts were much smaller than his pre-war yachts as a sign of the times. He maintained his captain, Captain Brow, but the days of luxurious cruising was over.

Source: Olds Family Archives – Ed Roe

In 1948, The **METTAMAR II** was built and delivered. It was a 57 foot Burger designed boat built in Manitowoc, WI. by the Burger Boat Company. Its beam was 14.5 feet and the draft was 4 feet. The yacht was equipped with twin 165hp G.M. diesel engines. There was 6 feet three inches of head room in the cabins.

The **METTAMAR II** was a steel yacht with 4 watertight bulkheads. She was fitted out with Honduras Mahogany. The yacht was well appointed and was used by Olds at his beloved Lake Charlevoix.

Source: Olds Family Archives – Ed Roe

The **METTAMAR II** underway on Lake Charlevoix, Michigan in late 1948.

Source: Olds Family Archives - Stephens

R.E. and Metta Olds on the **METTAMAR II**.

However, in 1949, the **METTAMAR II** was put up for sale. Below is the actual sales sheet for the cruiser.

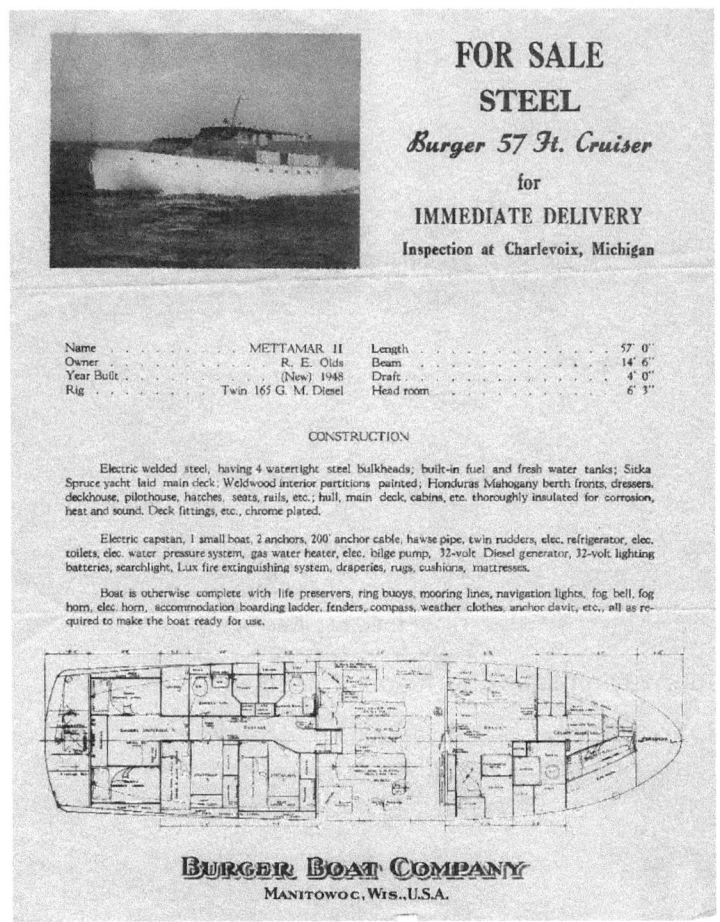

Source: Olds Family Archives - Stephens

Olds was too old to use the boat for a long cruise at this time in his life so his daughter, Gladys, took the boat from Hampton, VA. south for the winter. This boat was not the length nor carried the crew size of the earlier yachts. This trip was cruising, not yachting, with all the lack of creature comforts! The log book talks of the troubles and issues. The yacht experienced a series of mechanical problems as it went down the inland waterway (Intercoastal waterway today). Although Gladys purchased the boat from her father in 1948, it was soon put up for sale. It sold in 1949 and was renamed the **CHARLIS**. Records are not clear as when the next sale occurred but, the yacht was believed to have been sold in 1952 and renamed the **ALMARDON**. The fate of the **METTAMAR II** today is unknown.

Source: Olds Family Archives - Stephens

This painting of **REOLA III** was made by Constance Abel, a cousin of Metta Olds.

REOLA III was approximately 55 feet long. Olds only had this boat for 1 year starting in 1949 and traded it in for his final yacht, the **REOLA IV**. Olds sent a letter to Lloyd's Register in 1950 stating, in response to an inquiry, that he had turned the **REOLA III** in to the Burger Boat Company in May, 1950 for a larger boat. Little is known about this boat and it is possible that the family did not use it much. As we know, Olds was very specific about his yachts and if they did not suit him, then he simply ordered another built but with a different configuration or layout.

Source: Olds Family Archives - Stephens

REOLA IV was 58 feet. long. This yacht was delivered shortly before Olds' death in 1950. It too was built in Manitowoc, WI. by the Burger Boat Company. Letters in the family archives indicate the boat was kept for a short time after Olds' death. However, none of the heirs wanted to buy the boat. The cost of maintenance, carrying a crew and without Olds' robust outgoing spirit soon meant the glory boating days for the Olds family were in the past. Letters indicate the yacht was sold back to the Burger Boat Company in mid-1951. There are no records to indicate the eventual fate of **REOLA IV**.

Thus ended on August 26, 1950, with the death of R.E. Olds, a glorious chapter in yachting history. On the day he died, a number of family members were "up north" in Charlevoix. Rex Sessions of Lansing, Michigan, a longtime friend of the family, was at a house party at the Roe family cottage. Rex and a number of the younger generations were on the **REOLA IV** when Captain Brow boarded to tell them of the death of Olds and they should come into the cottage "in honor of Mr. Olds."

According to the inventory of his estate (*), Olds owned two boats at his death:
1) The **REOLA IV** (Burger built in 1950) valued at $55,000.
2) The **SEALARK** (Matthews built in 1937) valued at $7,500.

Source: Olds Family Archives – Stephens
R.E. Olds in his Matthews cruiser

The Matthew cruiser had a raised cabin but "otherwise it is standard throughout" according to R.E. Olds' note to a boat broker. The cruiser had a front stateroom with two berths. Aft of this was a head (toilet) and galley. Moving further aft, there was another stateroom one side and upper & lower berths on the other side. The after deck was approximately 10 feet long and was fitted with a folding table for four.

Nothing more is known about the Matthews or its power plant. Its eventual fate is unknown.

Like so many of his contemporary industrialists, Olds found yachting a refuge. For many of the other early industrials, it was a way to show their great wealth but for Olds it was less, much less, about the showcasing of wealth. For him, it was about family and friends. He loved being the grand host and one could probably assume, the center of attention! His ship's logs rarely carried the name of the wealthy and famous. His guests were his neighbors and friends from church along with his immediate family and scattered nephews and nieces.

During the process of this journey of discovery about R.E. Olds' yachts, it soon became apparent that Olds also had many smaller boats, such as launches and runabouts (see Chapter 6 for family photographs), most of which were not documented or recorded. There are some photographs of the other smaller boats but they tend to be more casual. Unfortunately we probably will never know about the true extent of his involvement in boating but the stories contained within about his yachts, and their eventual disposal, provide a fascinating glimpse into the life of one the Twentieth Century's most innovative and creative personalities.

For his love of yachting, he combined his creativity and engineering talents with leading designers of the day to create some of the America's most beautiful yachts with unique layouts and features. The family pictures give us a peek of a by-gone era. It is truly a shame that none of the yachts have survived throughout the years but the photographs show us a man completely content with his life and accomplishments. A man who was successful in many endeavors and shared his successes with others.

(*) In case you were curious, the following cars were owned by the auto pioneer at his death:
1) 1948 DeSoto Seven Passenger, valued at $1,235.
2) 1949 Chrysler Windsor sedan, valued at $1,645.
3) 1947 Oldsmobile Touring Sedan, valued at $1,074.

Your wealth is where your friends are.

Plautus

CHAPTER FIVE

Oldsmar:
acquired in 1916 and sold starting in 1923

Olds had long been interested in Florida real estate stemming from his early days of automobile racing on Florida beaches. He purchased property in Daytona in 1905 for his winter home and soon after took his first cruise on the rented yacht **ROCHESTER**. That led to the construction of his first yacht, the **REOPASTIME** which commenced cruising in 1907. With the growing economy, Olds was convinced his plans for a planned community were proper and well founded.

> Historical footnote: *The Daytona 500 races had their start in 1903 when Olds and his close friend, and competitor, Alexander Winton raced on the beach at Ormond Beach. For three decades, this beach was the place to race and test cars. The top speed in 1903 was an astonishing 68mph. By 1935, the speed had reached almost 300mph!*

Olds selected the site for his new city during previous yachting excursions to Florida. This site was selected for its location well to the north of Tampa Bay which Olds thought would protect boaters and residents from any potential hurricane damage. In fact, there was a town named Safety Harbor (incorporated in 1917) just down the bay from the site of Oldsmar. While it & Oldsmar might have been considered a "safe harbor" from storms, in fact the name Safety Harbor (derived from "safe harbor") had more to do with outrunning pirates that frequented the area in the early 1800's.

His vision of an idyllic warm weather setting coupled with a planned development that was focused upon families and community was an extension of his belief that there would be a growing and significant middle class. His view of a middle class, and the growing role of women, was quite unusual for its day. Rather than take a bully pulpit, he quietly went about his vision. He believed that time would prove him right, again, as he had shown with the small automobile. Olds did not lack for confidence.

From 1916 onward, Olds had further reduced his involvement in The REO Motor Car Company as he focused upon Oldsmar. Olds had correctly assumed the nation's economy would prosper and he wanted his grand experiment to be the vanguard for an enormous social experiment. Oldsmar, as a project, excited him as much as the early days of the automobile industry.

Olds was completely focused upon his considerable investment, both financial and philosophical, in Oldsmar, Florida. Like many of his peers, such as Flagler (Palm Beach) and Merrick (Coral Gables), Olds believed there was a fortune to be made in Florida real estate. Unlike those men who were building for people of similar wealthy financial means, Olds' plan was to establish a city for the working class, or as he was starting to envision, the new middle class.

In 1916, Olds purchased 37,451 acres from a Richard Peters. The price was $400,000 to be paid in $200,000 cash, $75,000 bonds and an apartment house in Daytona Beach worth $125,000. Olds created the REOLDS Farm Company to develop the property. The soon to be developed town was named discretely R.E. Olds-On-The-Bay but it was soon changed to Oldsmar.

Olds had planners, surveyors and architects from Boston develop a plan based upon Washington, D.C. with wide boulevards and streets. Olds was a large thinker and used to tackling seemingly impossible projects. This development would soon to be more than Olds could manage. Initially, he ran into numerous problems that he never contemplated. His simple resolution, like so many other things in his life, was to invent a solution. However, attracting companies and people to relocate to Oldsmar proved to be an entirely different matter. Here he used his marketing prowess to discuss upon the health benefits of living in the south and the improved standard of living one would have in Oldsmar. Olds also invested in companies as a way to entice them to Florida, like the Kardell Tractor Company. He even contacted President Woodrow Wilson to offer land for the government to build a shipbuilding plant. Olds was not shy about exploring ideas that could possibly complete his dream…and protect his investment.

The original plat map for Oldsmar showed a unique view of his vision. It had space on the outskirts of town for industrial plants and plots for residents to engage in small scale farming. A forty acre farm site could be cleared of brush and have new buildings for approximately $7,000 (or nearly $146,000 in 2017 dollars). The town was anchored by its waterfront and resort hotel, racetrack, boating, a thousand foot dock and a potential golf course. But the important feature was the ability for someone to purchase real estate with in a community that was designed for parks, recreation and commerce. All these amenities were to be easily accessible by the future Oldsmar residents. The **REOLA II** was his on-site yacht and office.

The late 1920's were a period of unprecedented prosperity. Personal income was rising and automobiles were becoming acceptable if not a necessity. This additional mobility led to the growth of what would become the modern suburb. The push for "good roads" also increased mobility as people could easily travel to formerly distant spots as a day trip. There was social and political changes as the national wealth nearly doubled. Unions, worker militancy, communism, socialism were all forming and growing.

However at the beginning of the 1920's, nearly half of the population of the United States was still agrarian based and struggling. World War I had caused US commodity prices to soar but the end of the war resulted in a catastrophe for farmers. With European farmers resuming farming, US wheat prices fell by nearly 50% and cotton prices by almost 75%. The crippling depression of 1921 was the worst deflation (18%) in 140 years. Whole sale prices fell by nearly 37% and the stock market declined by 47%. Whatever the post-World War I reasons for the economic decline (and they are numerous and still being debated today), it was a mercifully short decline and by 1923, the economy and employment was back on track.

Additionally, a significant hurricane in 1921 showed that Oldsmar was not a protected harbor that Olds assumed it was. It suffered great damage as the storms drove directly north into the Oldsmar development wreaking great havoc to property and land. Oldsmar itself was hit by a storm surge of nearly 14 feet above normal and suffered great devastation. The highest recorded wind gust was 140mph.

> **Historical footnote:** *The hurricane season of 1921 was a relatively inactive season. However, the third hurricane, the second and final major storm of the season, was the first major storm to hit Tampa Bay since 1848. It was a very destructive storm causing $10mm damage in 1921 or nearly $240mm in 2017 dollars. The winds were sustained at 75mph and there was a 10.5 foot storm surge in Tampa Bay.*

The damage was immense to the land and specifically to the Oldsmar project image. Olds' assumptions about the protective harbor for Oldsmar had been significantly in error. Oldsmar never recovered from the impact of that hurricane nor the effects of the 1921 depression. Olds continued to experience setbacks and a lack of interest. His special type of marketing, ranging from offering to build a shipyard for the US Navy during World War I to drilling an oil well and advertising "up north" did not pay off. Olds would continue to push Oldsmar for a few more years. His vision did not encompass the harsh realities of the time: a world war had just ended and a severe recession had damaged the finances and hopes of the people. Few people were willing to risk partaking in Olds' dreams when insecurity was already knocking on their doors.

Neither industry nor individuals moved to Oldsmar. However fortuitous timing was on Olds' side on his exit. Starting in 1923, Olds started to divest himself of his Oldsmar interests. He was essentially out of all but a small investment in Oldsmar by 1926. By 1925, the Florida real estate bubble was starting to unravel. A series of events showed the true speculative nature and size of the bubble. Two hurricanes (1926 and 1928) plus the stock market crash of 1929 finished off Florida real estate. Florida's economy would not recover until World War II. If Olds had not gotten out when he did, his losses would have been substantially greater. His timing on Florida real estate was way too early but his timing in cutting his losses was superb. Nonetheless, this dream cost him millions (tens of millions today).

A hundred years later, Oldsmar became exactly what he envisioned: a beautiful small town that is its own slice of heaven. But he was probably 50 years ahead of his time. The Oldsmar story is a fascinating view of Olds' multi-faceted talents and what could have been an amazing chapter in the American dream.

Olds lost, after liquidating the Oldsmar assets, nearly $3,000,000 of his personal fortune. Using the US Government's CPI Inflation calculator, this was the equivalent of nearly $44 million dollars in 2017. By 1923, Olds had nearly divested himself of all his Oldsmar investment.

OLDSMAR
FLORIDA

DEVELOPMENT BY
REOLDS FARMS CO.
LANSING, MICHIGAN
AND
OLDSMAR, FLORIDA

Source: R.E. Olds Transportation Museum

CHAPTER SIX
Family Photographs

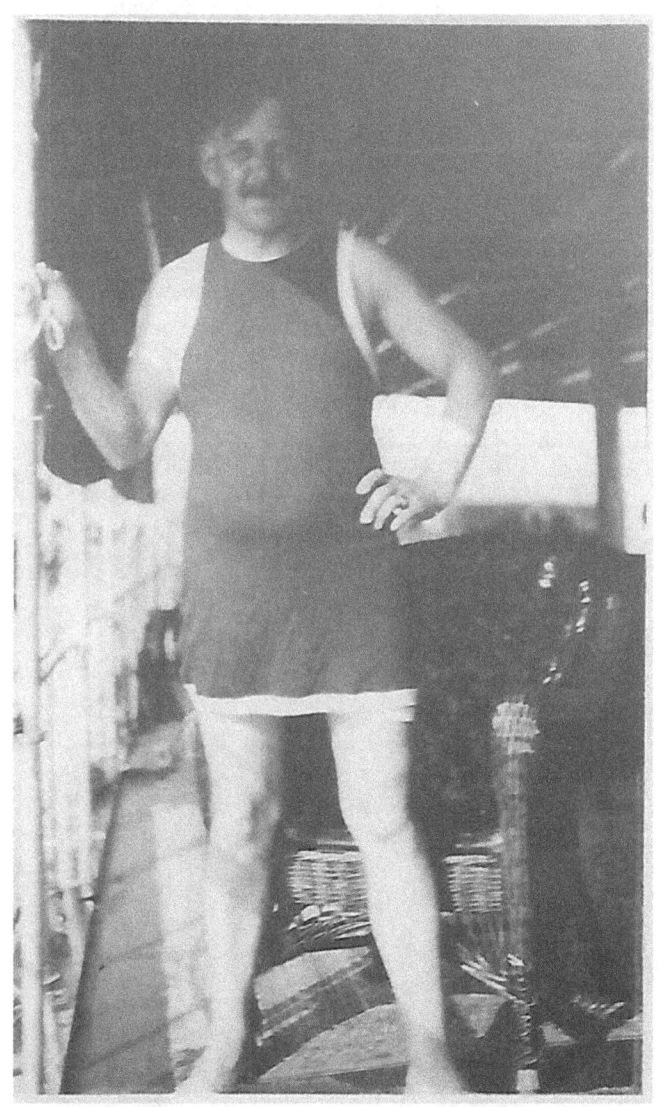

Source: Olds Family Archives - Stephens

R.E. Olds ready for a swim on the *REOMAR I*

Source: Olds Family Archives – Ed Roe

Oldswoode, the Olds family Chris Craft in Charlevoix, MI. R.E. Olds is driving the boat, Metta Olds is the passenger.

Source: Olds Family Archives – Stephens

Interior shot of the METTAMAR

Source: R.E. Olds Transportation Museum
METTAMAR under construction

Source: Olds Family Archives - Stephens

R.E. Olds (center) with his grandchildren and their friends

Source: Olds Family Archives – Stephens

R.E. Olds driving his runabout, **Oldswoode**. The picture is circa late 1930's.

Source: Olds Family Archives – Stephens

Olds grandchildren being pulled by the **REOMAR** IV yacht tender, driven by a crew member. The picture is circa mid-1930's.

Source: Olds Family Archives – Stephens

REOMAR IV napkin

Source: Olds Family Archives – Stephens
Laundry day on the **REOMAR IV**

Source: Olds Family Archives – Stephens
Olds launch at Elbamar, MI (circa 1920)

Source: Olds Family Archives – Stephens

Olds boathouse, Charlevoix, MI. (on left) for **REOMAR IV**

Source: Olds Family Archives - Stephens

Oldswoode (Chris Craft) runabout. R.E. Olds is sitting in the stern compartment

Source: Olds Family Archives - Stephens

R.E. & Metta Olds at Oldswoode on Lake Charlevoix, MI

Source: Olds Family Archives - Stephens

R.E. Olds on board the **REOMAR IV**

Source: Olds Family Archives - Stephens

Early Olds launch with a large group (before US Coast Guard regulations!) of women circa 1918; R.E. Olds is in the front with the straw hat.

Source: Olds Family Archives - Stephens
Gladys Olds, Oldest daughter of R.E. & Metta Olds. Picture taken circa 1920's.

Source: Olds Family Archives - Stephens

Launching the runabout from the *REOMAR I*

Source: Olds Family Archives - Stephens

R.E. Olds with his youngest daughter, Bernice. Photograph taken on the *REOMAR II*, circa 1914.

94 — Expense for August

			17.60
Aug	13	Carfare to Norfolk about Papers	20.00
	14	Groceries in Richmond for Crew	2.28
	16	Groceries in Norfolk for Crew	1.90
		Ice 1.00, Screws 15cts Paint & Brush 90cts	2.05
		Kerosene 25cts — Wipers for Engine 6.25	6.50
		Stamped Envelopes 53c	.53
	17	Meeles Reed Co 75cts — Pyrene 2.00	2.75
		Wood Shoots 3.00 Polish 3.00	6.00
		Groceries 1.96 Oil 3ny 10c	2.06
	18	Paid Steward 55.50	55.50
		Laundry 10.27	10.27
		Linoleum 13.60	13.60
		Groceries & per Bill	2.48
		White Enamel Paint	5.00
		Plane 50	.50
	19	J C Hurst 23.00 Pender 3.98	26.98
		Ice Box 5.00 Dishes for Crew 40cts	5.40
		Ice 1.05 Milk 30	1.35
	24	Groceries & Meat 2.28 Ice & Water 1.70	3.98
	26	Bread Potatoes & Meat 2.18 Machine Oil	2.18
	29	Groceries & Chicken 1.83	1.83
		Scrapers 30cts Ice 1.00	1.30
	31	Milk & Groceries 1.78	1.78
		Settled	173.67
Sept	1	Milk & Bread & Sausage 1.15	1.15
	2	Bread Sugar & Butter 1.34	1.34
		Sausage 20cts	.20
	3	Sapolio 50cts Fish 40cts Bacon 75cts	1.66
		Aluminium 50cts Meat 43cts	.93
	4	Potatoes 35cts 6 Chickens 2.00	2.35
		Fish 15cts Apples 25cts Cabbage 10cts	.50
		Gold Dust 10cts	.10
	5	Lard 45cts Fish 15cts Salmon 30cts	.90
			8.92

Source: Olds Family Archives - Stephens

August, 1915 Expense ledger for **REOLA II.** $173 is equal to $4,300 in 2018.

Source: Olds Family Archives – Stephens
Launch for the **REOMAR II**. Notice name on back seat. Photograph taken circa 1915.

Source: Olds Family Archives – Stephens
REOMAR I with all flags flying. Photograph taken in 1910.

Source: Olds Family Archives - Stephens

REOMAR II launch with a shore party. Photograph taken in 1910.

Source: Olds Family Archives - Stephens

Photograph taken on board **REOMAR II** in 1910. R.E. Olds in on the right. Notice the high-tech "sausage style" head preserver.

Source: 1896 Olds; New York Public Library Digital Collection; copyright unknown

Possibly the oldest known photograph of Olds' first internal combustion gasoline car. The photo states it was taken in 1896. The car appears to be running.

www.ingramcontent.com/pod-product-compliance
Lightning Source LLC
Chambersburg PA
CBHW081235170426
43198CB00017B/2769